C210163544

Made in
Nottingham

D1808533

Nottir
Cour

DP&P

Peter Mortimer's books
from Five Leaves include

Camp Shatila: a writer's chronicle

Off the Wall: the journey of a play

I Married the Angel of the North (poetry)

The Last of the Hunters: life with the fishermen of North Shields

Riot (a bilingual Arabic and English play text)

www.petermortimer.co.uk

Made in Nottingham
a writer's return

Peter Mortimer

Five Leaves Publications

Made in Nottingham
a writer's return
by Peter Mortimer

Published in 2012
by Five Leaves Publications,
PO Box 8786, Nottingham NG1 9AW
www.fiveleaves.co.uk

ISBN: 978-1907-869-52-5

Photo credits:
Tony Marson (front cover, modern photographs,
pages 12, 17, 29, 39, 113, 126, 173, 174, 181, 204)
Sue Dymoke (pages 195, 198)
Other photos courtesy of the author

Designed and typeset by
Four Sheets Design and Print

Five Leaves acknowledges financial support
from Arts Council England

Peter Mortimer would like to acknowledge
the financial assistance
of the Society of Authors

Printed in Great Britain
by Imprint Digital, Exeter

The past is like stuffed birds
which in our mind's eye
appear to fly
    SJ LITHERLAND

Breathes there the man with soul so dead
who never to himself has said
this is my own, my native land.
    SIR WALTER SCOTT
   (The Lay of the Last Minstrel, 6th Canto)

'Hiraeth' (Welsh) — a powerful yearning
for the place you came from
  (no equivalent word in English)

The way to the past is never smooth
    EAVAN BOLAND

*This book is for the life and work
of the Nottingham novelist,
Stanley Middleton*

FOREWORD

The Mortimer family left Sherwood council estate, Nottingham, in 1963 when I was 19. My mother, Mary Leddy, ('Minny' to everyone) had travelled from County Cavan in rural Ireland as an 18 year old to train as a nurse in Nottingham, and got to know my father Alex Mortimer when nursing him in hospital. He was a shop assistant from a working-class Nottingham family. Post-war, our family of four (including my brother Alex, two years older than me) lodged in a few 'digs' which I can scarcely recall, before moving onto the estate around 1947.

I was well into teenage years when my father sought out horizons beyond the shop counter, aspiring to be upwardly mobile — not that anyone had heard the phrase then. Around 1960 he set up his own one-man business buying hosiery wholesale from Nottingham manufacturers, and selling it direct to the public below the full retail price. He did this via classified adverts placed in newspapers around the country. Customers would send postal orders when ordering. Postal orders, for the benefit of any young readers, are like cheques, but you don't need a bank account to use them.

The business eventually became one man plus an occasional youth. In the evenings I'd help parcel up the stockings (this was pre-tights era) in the back room of our Sherwood council house, and my dad would take them the next day to the post office. I suspect this commercial dealing was illegal on domestic council property.

My father had a determined streak to forge his own fate. He deliberately neutered his Nottingham accent, joined a golf club, and as soon as the business showed signs of success, rented an office and small warehouse in nearby Arnold, selling hosiery and knitwear not only to the public but also to shops. Brother Alex was also proving himself upwardly mobile. He was academically

7

bright, and one of the few lads growing up on a council estate to pass Latin and Ancient Greek at A-level. Alex broke the mould of working-class lads from Sherwood Estate, applied to, and was accepted by Manchester University, an achievement that elevated him to almost heroic status in the eyes of me and his other mates. Such institutions for us were as distant as the moon.

The Mortimers were on the move. In 1963 the family upped sticks from Sherwood Estate to a big posh house in Redhill on the northern outskirts of Nottingham, where my dad swanked round in a Jaguar XJ6. Eventually he had his own brand of knitwear. I was on the move too — downwards. I got the sack from my first job — this was such an unlikely vocation that when much later I came to work as a writer in schools I offer £100 to any pupil who could guess it and the bet has never been won. I was employed as a trainee false-teeth salesman for the Nottingham dental firm of Arthur E. Inger Ltd, where in reality my tasks never graduated beyond wrapping up packs of false teeth and other dental requirements in the basement. These were posted off to dental surgeries throughout the Midlands. Regular enquiries to my employers as to when my exciting life on the road would begin brought no concrete response. After 18 months, I grew bored and sullen, a resentment which led to me doing even this menial job badly. Parcels were misposted; dentures intended for Leicester pensioners ended up in the mouths of blast furnace workers in Corby. I was given the sack. I had little direction or ambition, applied for several other jobs, and was turned down by all of them.

My father offered me work as a salesman, lugging samples round small drapers' shops in the East Midlands. This was marginally better than wrapping false teeth, though for the shop owners I was often the tenth rep of the day, all selling similar stuff, so the welcome wasn't always open-armed. Being pretty gobby, I charmed enough shop-keepers to keep the order book healthy. I was a shallow youth, interested mainly in football, drink and females, and for various reasons this mini 'family firm' set-up was always doomed to failure. My father and I were different animals.

The uncomfortable working relationship reached crisis point one evening when we stood up and exchanged blows at home over the evening meal. I scuttled away to lick my wounds and hatched a secret plan. By this time my brother Alex was pursuing his academic career at Manchester, where I'd occasionally visit him, envying what I saw as a student life of parties and women. This apparent hedonism contrasted sharply with my own existence: trussed up in a sober suit, driving round to spout false bonhomie to a succession of dreary drapers, the evenings spent in our house of tensions and bad silences on what I saw as a snotty-nosed private cul-de-sac, removed from my real friends, all of whom still lived on Sherwood Estate, a place my father had now turned his back on.

I decided to apply for university myself, a decision totally unrelated to academic striving. I said nothing to my parents until the letter of acceptance came. I never gave a thought as to their feelings.

Naturally my first choice was Manchester, who had the good sense to turn me down. Sheffield University accepted me and an entire new life was about to begin. My degree would be a BA in Economics. I had no particular love of economics, and had studied French and German at A-level. But when I left school, my father, keen to see me advance in the commercial world which he believed was my natural home (even though I was only wrapping up false teeth in a basement), insisted I should study for the Higher National Certificate in Business Studies, to which I devoted three nights and one full day a week for three years. This, plus my four years work experience, stood me in good stead as a 'mature student' (a not totally accurate description) for a place in the social sciences, which in the Sixties was an area of huge academic expansion. Plus which, four years after A-levels, my

9

A good school report, sadly not typical

French and German were a bit rusty compared with fresh-cheeked youngsters straight from school.

I left Nottingham in 1965 for Sheffield, and within a year a new energy appeared in my life — writing. Like many adolescents I wrote reams of dreadful poems, most of them sub-Bob Dylan. These I typed out and pinned to the wall in my bedsit, planning to show them to all female visitors who would be so overwhelmed as to abandon themselves to me instantly. Only occasionally did this work. Unlike many adolescents, my writing bug didn't fade away. I set up a literary magazine, contributed to the students' periodical, and when I graduated, wrote to 23 separate newspapers before getting a job as a reporter on the *Walthamstow Guardian* in East London, where on day one I was despatched to a story about a cat up a tree.

After two years I moved to Newcastle to work on the North-East morning newspaper, *The Journal*, where nine years later I gave up full-time journalism to concentrate on my own work — plays, poetry, editing a small press, children's writing, peripatetic books, and a life of low-income freedom I enjoy to this day.

Sheffield was my road to Damascus, and my life was changed radically thereafter.

For the first time in my life I knew what I was fated to do. This knowledge has been a bulwark through all manner of hardships, and I am deeply grateful for it. Creative artists have a luxury denied to many: their work is not only of choice, but also (if they're genuine) of passion. For this reason they shouldn't be over-bothered about being rich in monetary terms. On Sherwood Estate, a future life of writing for a living had not appeared an option, even though back in my first year at grammar school, I won a prize for storytelling, more of which later. At that time I made no connection between this and my life to come. Ambition was defined mainly via dreams of playing in the next World Cup. For the record, this did not take place.

Now, from what seemed like a distance of several galaxies, I planned to return to Sherwood Estate and Nottingham, to live a month just a few doors from where a previous version of Mortimer spent the often errant years of his youth. This prospect both challenged and disturbed me, a fear that I may be unearthing some undead George Romero creature, some grotesque spectre from a previous life, best left buried by history.

I sent a letter to my former address marked, 'The Occupants, 97 Danethorpe Vale, Sherwood Estate, Nottingham'. I wrote the envelope by hand, hoping thereby it wouldn't simply be thrown away as junk mail, explaining who I was and my plan for a temporary return to the estate. The mere act of writing that address, familiar yet long buried, sent a charge through me.

Three days later, I answered the phone. It was a female voice, that flat Nottingham accent rarely heard outside the

East Midlands and never quite managed by actors. "Hello, this is Valerie Mead of 85 Danethorpe Vale, Sherwood'.

Hearing the words 'Danethorpe Vale' sent another high voltage charge through me. Even at this early stage, I felt my long-lost past looming out of the mist, and was unsure whether to welcome or fear it. With those few spoken words a door was opened on the past that could not easily be closed. The words were a proclamation, a challenge, a seductive entreaty. I knew from that moment there was no going back. And yet that was exactly what I was planning to do.

Valerie Mead and her partner Derrick lived at 85 Danethorpe Vale, six doors up from the house where I grew up. But there was a family connection between the two houses, hence them replying to my letter. Number 97 was owned by Derrick, who once lived there prior to his relationship with Valerie. It was now occupied by his thirty-two year old son, also called Derrick, who'd been born in the house.

85 Danethorpe Vale today

"You wouldn't want to stay there," said Valerie down the phone, "Young Derrick never has anyone in that house. But you can come and live here."

This was disarmingly generous, given our briefest of acquaintance via the telephone. "Maybe I could come down to see you next week?" I said.

I had a plan. On the Tuesday evening, Notts County were at home to Lincoln City, and if they won, would be promoted for the first time in twelve years. I had supported County from the age of four, after being beaten up by a big lad sporting a red and white Nottingham Forest scarf. Most of those years were spent watching County struggle against relegation or sliding ever further into the shadow of the more glamorous Forest, who not that long since had won the European Cup for two successive years, a prospect for County about as remote as the Yorkshire Ripper being knighted.

I still saw the team occasionally when they played in the North East but had not visited their Meadow Lane ground for several years. It had been transformed from a rickety terraced wooden structure into a neat 24,000 all-seater stadium. County attracted crowds of around 6,000 as against the 20,000-plus of Forest.

It was forty-five years since I'd left the city, yet there in the Match Day programme was a familiar name, Colin Slater, who had been writing about Notts County for half a century and whose match reports and team news in *The Nottingham Evening Post* I read avidly almost fifty years ago. Finding his column was strangely reassuring, that deeply conservative, and dangerous, desire to know nothing has changed.

Nearly 8,000 turned up to the game that night; it was a charged atmospheric experience. County won 3-1, and each time they scored I had a rush of pure ecstasy, an instant soaring to giddy heights. I hear people get this from a snort of coke, but football's cheaper, and sometimes less damaging. I realised, no matter how much I watched and supported Newcastle United, or my local

Northern league team, Whitley Bay, no matter how many years I had been distant, Notts County is *my* team. Only Notts County could produce the extreme palpitations, the tremors, the abject gloom, the soaring elation, the behavioural patterns that totally mystified my partner Kitty and others. Football was no longer the life-and-death affair of my youth. There was too much else to life, and 5pm Saturday was no longer sacrosanct as results time. But the Lincoln game affirmed I was emotionally hardwired into Notts County FC. And that was a constant.

It was also illogical. None of those wearing the black and white shirts that night had the remotest connection to my own Nottingham. Within a few years most of them, as is the wont of football mercenaries, would be earning their crust with other clubs. Player-club loyalty was as ephemeral as clouds. As individuals I knew nothing about them. None of this mattered a damn. At the final whistle, as the County players ran up to salute us noisy fans, I was, ridiculously, in tears.

I stayed that night in Mapperley with my publisher Ross Bradshaw, and slept fitfully, partly due to the emotion of Meadow Lane, the Notts County ground, partly the prospect of walking the next morning through Sherwood Estate, less than two miles distant.

Danethorpe Vale stretches the length of the estate (approximately half a mile), the only thoroughfare to do so. It runs from Mansfield Road at the top, down to Valley Road at the bottom. Sherwood Estate sits on a north-facing hill, an early council estate (work began in 1920) built before the upsurge in car ownership and not particularly suited to modern excesses of traffic. As elsewhere, Margaret Thatcher's 1980 initiative to offer council houses for sale had seen about half the properties bought by the tenants. Thus the previous uniformity of paint colour and architecture was broken by an extension, a new porch, fancy gates or walls. A few FOR SALE signs were in evidence. The estate was much greener than I recalled.

At this stage, I was seeing Sherwood Estate not in cold reality but through some distorting prism, some atavistic throwback. A former version of myself was walking through a 45-year-old dream. Images, memories, voices, smells crowded in on me. We'd built a bonfire on that piece of grass; I'd grabbed a clumsy grope from a lass by that gate; we used to sledge down that hill; the mad woman we all feared had lived locked away just there; I'd kicked a football through that window and run off.

Despite the odd cosmetic changes, Sherwood Estate still felt like Sherwood Estate. And the past, at that moment, was infinitely more powerful than the present. This was a dangerous state of affairs anywhere, at any time. It would need to change during my month back in Nottingham. And documenting that change was likely to be at the centre of my writing, and could well be painful.

Valerie Mead was a retired teacher and her partner Derrick Olner a retired roofer. Both had been previously married. Derrick's wife had died of cancer and Valerie was divorced. Their three-bedroomed house, which

Valerie Mead and Derrick Olner

15

Valerie had purchased prior to their relationship, was comfortable and tidy. There were chickens in the back garden and Valerie had once kept goats (large gardens were considered an essential on many early council estates). The roof sported solar panels, and the spare bedroom was spacious, with a double bed, enough room for a writing table, and a view directly onto Danethorpe Vale itself. I began to feel at home.

If such details were reassuring, the view of number 97, six doors down, was less so. Derrick Junior lived there alone. The untended garden was full of old chairs and rubbish, the hedge, high and wild, blotting out the world. The curtains were drawn, the paint was sad and peeling, the window cracked. A dividing fence now separated what had once been the common path through to the back with number 99. The house I grew up in looked to be breathing its last, dying on its feet. It was crying out for care and attention. For no logical reason, a rush of guilt took hold of me, as if the house's wretched state were my own fault, as if for all those years I should have been there to protect it, as if no house in your life could ever be as important as the one in which you grew up.

I had taken myself off, gadded around the country and the world with hardly a second thought for the house. And now it was expiring. I knew that some way, however painful, at some time during my stay, I had to go inside 97 Danethorpe Vale, though I said nothing at that time to either Valerie or Derrick. Inside that house was Derrick's son, and an entire story of which I was thus far ignorant. And at that moment I could not have predicted how my feelings to my one-time home would eventually change.

It would be another year before I travelled down to live at 85 Danethorpe Vale. Various complications brought delays, but by April 2011, with Notts County once again facing the familiar situation of a relegation battle, I was ready to up sticks from the familiarity of Tyneside, and plonk myself down into the once intimate, yet now alien world of Sherwood Estate, where almost half a century

97 Danethopre Vale today

had passed since my life there, a time-span of almost unbridgeable proportions.

And what exactly did I expect to achieve or to prove? What was my ambition, my goal? I had few answers, except a strong instinct that told me to return, and from the experience, discover some context, something of relevance. To make sense of things — that urge that drives writers on. Predictably, as the date of departure approached, so too did the sense of disturbance and insecurity; Peter Mortimer of the present travelling down the murky road to Peter Mortimer of the past, two people who may have nothing in common. Inside my head, no matter how I tried to convince myself otherwise, I regularly heard the whispered maxim that you could never go back. So what on earth was this journey all about?

FORGET MEMORY

Forget memory.
Things are not as you recall
and the dead, when woken
are never quite themselves.

If you insist that memory
pays you a visit, keep it short.
Sit memory by the fire
offer it light refreshments
allow it brief time for anecdotes
stories, bitter-sweet recalls.

That Greek island — ah!
That winning goal — yes!
The playing fields of youth — indeed!

Then glance at your watch
hand memory its hat and coat
and say, "Well, I'm sure you've things to do.
I know I have."

Somewhere is a small voice.
The voice of people who have gone
places that are no more
events that have passed on.
Listen hard. The voice is whispering
"Do not dwell long on us.
Let us go. Let us go."

Meantime a knock comes at the door.
Do not shout, "I am busy with memory!"
The knock may not return
may leave you in silence
folded into an old armchair
staring through a grimy window
at streets you can no longer walk.

TUESDAY APRIL 19

THE HISTORY MAN AND THE GHOST

Had I been a follower of omens, I may well have had second thoughts early on. A sore throat and husky voice set in three weeks before departure, and I couldn't shake it off, leaving me a perfect contender to cut a blues album, but slightly dysfunctional otherwise. The doctor diagnosed laryngitis, bunged me the obligatory antibiotics, and when I nervously mentioned the possibility of throat cancer, instead of laughing uproariously, offered the barely reassuring 'Not very likely. Come back if it doesn't clear up.'

My friend, the actor Annie Orwin, recommended lots of water plus three days of complete silence. The latter, requiring a Trappist monk-style discipline, proved unfeasible for a loud-mouth such as myself. The condition only partially cleared up, and later in the year I needed two throat operations for a condition called severe dysplasia which I'd never heard of (cells on the vocal cords) but which, at time of writing, appears to have gone away.

I did stay silent while packing my large trunk, a symbolic act, as back in 1965 this very trunk had first carried me and my possessions away from Nottingham. It was a present from my parents (were they trying to tell me something?) with my initials PJGM embossed in gold on the side. Now, when I opened the trunk lid, I breathed in aromas which instantly carried me back to distant times; moth balls, airing cupboards, the smells of yesteryear.

The second possible omen was when I drove up to the entrance of the Tyne Tunnel. I had piled my month's necessities into my partner Kitty's car, a small four-wheel drive which she generously lent me. It was rush hour, the second Tyne Tunnel was being built, the huge road works each end bringing 24-hour jams. I stuck the £1.20 toll in the barrier, the bar lifted, but the car refused to budge. Within fifteen seconds the queue behind was tailing back towards Edinburgh, and the symphony of the honking horns had begun. I tried again; loud revving, but no movement.

To the attendant who came running over, I croaked as best I could, "Sorry, it won't budge."

"Pardon?"

"I said it won't budge." (My voice was now at 50 per cent).

At such moments you felt an incompetent idiot (a tautologous phrase). I was not a man much given to indulging in automotive products, nor did I see driving or cars as more than an occasionally necessary tedium. A night out with Jeremy Clarkson was not on my wish list.

The burly attendant pushed the car through the barrier into a siding where I discovered for some reason the motor had jumped out of two-wheel drive. I remembered something about engaging two- or four-wheel drive, found a button marked 2 and pressed it. The sweet tones of Radio Two sounded out, soothing enough, but of little help in restoring mobility. I found another number 2 button and pressed that. The vehicle now responded, and I drove off through the tunnel fearful the fault may re-occur. Breaking down inside the Tyne Tunnel at rush hour was not only less advisable than standing outside St. James Park, Newcastle on match day shouting "all Geordies are bastards!", it also incurred a fine roughly equivalent to the Greek national debt. Happily the rest of the journey was uneventful.

It was a beautifully warm sunny day, clement weather conditions that would persist throughout my stay. Whatever else, Nottingham was to give me almost unlimited sunshine. As the fabled city grew closer I began again to ask myself what I was doing. My writing was not

21

particularly autobiographical; I'd always favoured quarrying the imagination rather than my own life story for ideas. I had a sneaking admiration for the Gore Vidal comment that 'write about what you know' was lazy advice handed out by creative writing teachers for students unwilling or unable to make much of an imaginative journey.

Few of my friends or family made their way into my poems or plays. In an age when people assiduously researched family trees and traced their ancestry back to Ethelred the Unready, I was shamefully ignorant on the history of either the Mortimer or the Leddy family. This had not caused me much lack of sleep. I was wary of the past's hold on us, and generally was in sympathy with the Buddhist persuasion on the importance of the moment. Yet here I was, voluntarily driving through a time warp, not on some brief nostalgic visit, but to plonk myself down month-long in a world I had known almost half a century ago and one which until this day had been more or less safely buried.

In 48 years, despite various visits to my parents' post-Sherwood Nottingham homes, I had not once ventured onto Sherwood Estate. That chapter of my life, I told myself, was ended. And now I was turning the car into Danethorpe Vale, Sherwood Estate. I had never driven a car along these streets. How disconnected it felt, how small the estate seemed, where once it had embraced almost my entire universe. I parked outside number 85. How odd Kitty's modern vehicle looked, as if it had just time-slipped 48 years into the past. Yet what a pleasant aspect the house offered on this warm spring day. The front garden boasted a host of trees: the shimmering yellow leaf of an acer, the delicate pink blossom of two cherry trees, a eucalyptus, and a rowan. Not that I knew the names of them all, but Valerie Mead did.

And if the estate seemed small, the gardens were more spacious than remembered, a testament to the new public housing policy at the start of the 20th century which

22

believed an essential for working people was space and room to breathe, so that both front and back no Sherwood estate house looked cramped or confined and greenery was in profusion.

Valerie answered the door, probably as nervous as myself, but we greeted one other warmly. A cup of tea was the first essential, followed immediately by a sandwich bulging with cold beef, the first indication that a man would not go hungry in this house. The back room housed a large TV, a settee, one arm-chair, a narrow glass-fronted bookcase, neutral colour walls, mainly unadorned, and a French window looking out onto a small open patio. The terraced garden rose up in small sections, the view of most of which was blocked by high hedges.

There was only one tiny table in this room. I sat down in the armchair which immediately, and by unspoken agreement, became mine for the month.

My bedroom had been cleaned and prepared by Valerie, though the desire to root myself and cast off the feelings of uncertainty meant I had to personalise it via some readjustments. I laid out my writing gear: notebooks lap-top, ink and reference books, turning the small table as much as possible into a desk. I unpacked everything, marked out my territory, creating the sense of a bedsit. When I first escaped Nottingham I lived as a student in a Sheffield bedsit, and was so intoxicated with the sense of freedom that I have been required to recreate that same liberation ever since, wherever the location. My entire life prior to leaving Sherwood Estate was spent sharing a bedroom with my brother Alex, thus the luxury of any territory I could call my own was unknown. Self-expression began with having my own room. And having my own room meant not having a bed in the centre.

With a certain sense of ceremony, I pushed the bed against the corner wall.

Derrick was not in. I had little plan, except knowing the first essential was to walk round the estate. I stood

23

outside the gate of number 85, and found myself frozen in memory. I could not move. The past had turned me to stone. Which direction? Right would take me up Danethorpe Vale to the top of the estate. Left would take me to my previous home, number 97. To go up Bonnington Crescent opposite would take me a long curving route that eventually dropped me down towards Valley Road. These were simply roads, buildings, hedges. These were places people lived and walked and got on with life. They were not history, nor where ghosts loomed on every corner. People did not wake up daily on this estate and see spectres rise before them.

Yet here were those very spectres for me. Looking to the left I conjured up the amiable Ron Duffin, the bread delivery man, walking from his gate, brushing the few strands of thinning hair across his head; I saw the stern Mr Breen come down his path and admonish us for once again booting the football into his garden; I saw old Mr Mundin push his antediluvian bike down his path, and with great effort heave his bulky frame onto it, wobbling away at painfully slow speed, looking for all the world like a sack of spuds. To the right I saw Mrs Skinner, as skinny as a hairgrip, body curved to the shape of a banana, thin white hair like a cloud of cigarette smoke, gossiping as she would gossip daily at the bottom of Danethorpe Vale.

I saw these people, yet none of them had been there for decades. I was viewing this estate through a distorted prism, and at that moment a huge sadness weighed down on me, a genuine doubt that I would be able to see this month through. It was as if I were part of some terrible joke, or a science fiction story where I had been dropped into the estate of my childhood, sealed in a time bubble of whose existence every other person was unaware, yet which would render me non-functional.

I told myself such thoughts simply would not do, and willed one leg to move in front of the other. I strode up Bonnington Crescent, admonishing myself. I passed the odd person on the pavement, in a garden, or driving slowly

24

past in a car. Unlike me, none seemed weighed down with a lead-filled suitcase of memory and history.

Though the estate was open and spacious, the roads themselves, mainly curvy, were not wide, unlike the pavements. They were from an age when walkers were given as much preference, if not more, than those behind a wheel. The trend to render pedestrians less important than motorists would reach its zenith (nadir?) with the construction of the motorways on which the act of walking was simply illegal.

Many of the houses were now privately owned. A few had ostentatious black iron gates, trimmed with even more ostentatious gold. Several lawns had been sacrificed to ugly slab paving to allow parking space. The lawns that survived were rarely neatly trimmed, yet not running amok. Hedges also were only partially tamed, as if the excessive tidiness of a private suburban estate was not wanted here. The most neglected hedge on the whole estate, I was soon to discover, was the one at 97 Danethorpe Vale. Despite privatisation, few houses had been given names, suggesting the naming of houses was a strictly middle-class pursuit.

My first shock came when approaching the estate's one-time main open space, Collin Green. This had been a large open circle of grass, surrounded by railings. In my childhood Collin Green was witness to estate lads playing more or less constant football. Among the players regularly shooting between two sets of coats, were three youngsters destined to become full professionals, an elevation guaranteeing almost deific status among us mere mortal contemporaries. More of them later.

This one-time nurturing ground for the young footballer was now a circle of flats for the elderly, built and designed to look inwards to a small landscaped garden, as if age brought a necessary restriction of vision and horizons, and all looking outward was done for.

It would take me some time to shake off a sense that such developments were unnatural, unjust intrusions on

25

the true order, an interference with what had been the 'proper' state of affairs — that which pertained in my own day. I was clinging on to the past and the belief that on Sherwood Estate it was more relevant than the present-day. This was a debilitating trait which could cause nostalgic inertia, and I needed to watch out.

I passed a small electricity substation on whose metal fencing was fixed a brass plaque with the words, *In Loving Memory of Jason Spencer, 6th March 2007, Gone but Never Forgotten,* and suspended close by an old-fashioned lantern and candle. A comforting thought — that we were never forgotten. But already on Sherwood Estate I sensed I was totally forgotten. It was some weeks later I discovered who Jason Spencer had been.

How quiet the estate was on this sunny day. How green. What huge significance these moments had for me. Yet for those few people I saw, the moments were of little consequence, and would be rapidly forgotten. In all my years in Sherwood, I had never thought it odd that the main estate boasted not a single shop, public house, community centre, library, church, police station, no bus route, nor any other amenity. I did recall a small newsagent in Edingey Square, part of the western offshoot area, severed from the main estate by the busy Edwards Lane. The newsagent was now gone.

Plonking myself down for a month in a house of total strangers was an act of faith, both for Derrick and Valerie but also myself. It was a situation fraught with potential problems. I suspected their lives and my life were very different, culturally and socially. All three of us had taken on the arrangement virtually blind. Now for four weeks we would be living at close quarters, exposed not only to possible ideological contrasts but (perhaps more important) those minor domestic differences that could drive people to murder.

In these first days, Valerie gently reminded me not to leave a mug of tea perched on the side of the armchair, pointed out my casually tugged shower curtain was

26

failing to prevent water leaking onto the bathroom floor, and hinted I might ensure the garden gate was closed to prevent errant dogs wandering in. Catching her brushing up spots of soil from the carpet, I realised shoes were rarely worn round the house, and thereafter removed my big clumpy boots on entry.

On the other side, I requested Valerie not to add milk to my tea before taking out the tea bag, an indulgence that could lose me the will to live; I grew exasperated with the kitchen's tiny swing-bin whose busted lid regularly fell off, and bought a larger, sturdier replacement from Wilkos in Sherwood, hoping this would not be seen as interference. We survived these hiccups, just as we survived our conflicting opinions on the forthcoming wedding of William and Kate.

I also grew used to the norm of eating each meal from a tray watching TV. Radios did not feature at 85 Danethorpe Vale except for a 'Shower Radio' in the bathroom which had a liking for Five Live, but little interest in receiving other stations. Being a radio addict, I had with me a small set of my own, but it proved resistant on Sherwood estate to both my favourites, Radio Four and Radio Three, while BBC Radio Nottingham beamed loud and clear. Thus my radio diet pattern here differed from the norm.

Food was plentiful and traditional. In the second week, I offered to cook, and did so twice, while accepting Valerie's reminder that Derrick enjoyed the basics. "He's not that gone on foreign food," she confided. Derrick didn't spend much time in the kitchen either cooking or washing up, and as far as I could tell did little of the food shopping.

On this night the grub was chicken, chips and peas, two thick slices of buttered white bread and a mug of tea. Derrick was bald on the top, with a shock of hair sprouting from the sides. He had the broadest Nottingham accent; the vowels and intonation in these early days of my Nottingham rehabilitation often seemed like an

27

exaggeration done for humorous effect, so that without intention, people sounded comic. I was reminded how little-known the Nottingham accent was outside the East Midlands, and for the first time in years heard such words as 'bogger' (bugger), and 'tuffy' (sweet); a bread roll was a 'cob', and a term of affection was to call someone 'me duck'.

There was of course the matter of my previous home, 97 Danethorpe Vale. "Has Derrick Junior said anything about letting me in the house?" I asked Valerie and Derrick Senior. They both shook their heads. "It's really important I get inside number 97," I continued. "Hardly anyone goes into that house," said Derrick.

"I grew up there," I said. "You'll just have to ask young Derrick," said Valerie, "If you can catch him."

I took another walk to stand outside number 97, and again felt a great sadness at the dilapidated appearance. It was probably the most rundown house on the estate.

I considered walking up the overgrown path and knocking on the faded paint of the door. For the second time that day on Sherwood Estate, my body was immobile with indecision. After a few seconds I walked away. I knew it was a step too far, knew I first needed to talk to Derrick Jnr. I was confident of my persuasive powers.

All three pubs I'd frequented as a teenager were just outside the estate boundaries; at the top southern extremity was The Garden City (now renamed The Sherwood Manor). This impressive white building with imposing pillared entrance, would not look out of place on a Deep South plantation. Only now did I learn the pub had been built to celebrate the founding of the estate, the name Garden City conveying the urban/green mix of the new development. Just beyond the north-east end of Valley Road was the eye-catching art deco structure, The Vale Hotel, and the third, The Five Ways, was a half-timbered 1913 Grade Two listed building at the Valley Road/Edwards Lane roundabout, which does in fact offer five exits. That pub is visible from the bottom of Dane-

thorpe Vale. I never gave a single thought to the unique architecture of this trio during my Sherwood days. They were simply places to drink in.

I was thankful all three were still open. Nationwide, we have the anomaly of drunkenness ever rising while pubs close at an accelerating rate. One reason is the hugely discounted supermarket booze, which meant many weekend tipplers are well bladdered from home consumption by the time they step onto licensed premises, where consequently they spent less loot.

The Five Ways had been my main watering hole. In this establishment I had learnt to drink, to play darts and dominoes. I had mixed with older men outside of family and work, and had taken from them both wisdom and stupidity. In the main, young men now drank with other young people in bars whose loud music, flashing lights and banks of video screens were marketed to attract only the one age range, so the wisdom and stupidity they learned from this narrow group was less useful than mine.

I had drunk in the Five Ways from an early age; one night when I stood a round of drinks, the landlord asked me the reason for the celebrations and I said, "My eighteenth birthday." He answered, "Yo cheeky young bogger!" The landlord's name was Dick Randall, and his portly appearance earned him the nickname of Moby Dick, which was never said to his face. His daughter was more than tasty but always out of reach for us estate lads.

Inside, The Five Ways had changed little. Its special status had seen it spared the fate of many pubs, which have been turned into interior designers' identikit barns. You entered a pleasant wood-panelled corridor from which all bars were accessed. This area itself offered a bar space where it turned at right angles towards the second door. This corridor section had tables and chairs, and was often the clientèle's favourite grazing area. If we count this as a room, then the pub boasted five of the same. The panelled doors into the individual bars retained their original ornate glass signs, and the pub sign itself, a traveller carrying his possessions in a spotted scarf on a stick, and resting with his dog against a Celtic Cross where five roads met, was also, if memory served me, the same as half a century ago.

The Five Ways was now owned by Punch Taverns, and had been run for ten years by Steve and Yvette Miller. Each Monday it had a public auction, Slimmers' World met on Thursday, there were karaoke nights, the large concert room had regular jazz sessions, including one that night, frequented by a small group of elderly men; you could book a wedding 'do' for a grand, and the Sherwood Room had a pool table. Despite these activities, it rarely seemed busy. Bingo was being played this evening, a smattering of players scattered through the premises, and the calling by the barman was perfunctory; such adornments as, "Two and six — was she worth it?" or, "Eighty-eight, two fat ladies" being absent from the utilitarian repertoire.

I had last drunk, and been drunk, in this pub as a teenager. I was now 67, an oddly unsettling statistic. Had I expected merely to sidle in, pull up a seat and carry on as normal? I chatted that night briefly to Steve and Yvette Miller, and exchanged a few words with the barman and the odd customer, but to say lifelong friendships were forged would be excessive. I was to visit The Five Ways several times, but discerning readers will note how on each visit I felt increasingly peripheral, more removed.

As the present slowly pushed out the past, and as I struggled between the extremes of wanting to banish history, and keep it identical to what it was, so my presence in The Five Ways seemed increasingly unnatural, as if I no longer belonged. Which of course I didn't. Sitting by the bar in that corridor brought back a bitter-sweet anecdote recounted by my father. Sometimes he would drink in The Five Ways public bar with his friend Stan, a handsome and elegantly dressed man, funny, generous and something of a hero to us lads. He lived with his family a few doors up on Danethorpe Vale, and was forging out a successful executive career with the Nottingham textile manufacturer Bairnswear. Once Stan and his family tasted this success, they moved off the estate to a posh house in nearby Woodthorpe, a piece of upward mobility which I suspect further motivated my father in his own desire to climb the social scale.

The two men would drink two or three pints, during which time Stan would make regular trips to the toilet via the aforementioned wooden-panelled corridor. My father couldn't understand how Stan seemed to get pretty drunk pretty quickly, unaware of Stan's arrangement with the barman to have a double whisky (which he would down in one gulp, *en passant*), positioned on that same corridor bar for every loo visit. Unknown to friends and family, at that time Stan was already sliding into the alcoholism which would eventually destroy him. Among my most painful memories was when, some years later on

31

a trip to Nottingham, a mate pointed out a dishevelled tramp sat in a corner in The Garden City, hunched over his drink.

"That's Stan," he said. The metamorphosis from dapper heroic figure into forlorn wretch was earth-shattering, and for the first time in my life I was aware of the ravages of alcohol. I went to speak to Stan, but was unsure how much he remembered me. He seemed hardly to connect. Stan died not long after, but that final image of the dishevelled tramp haunts me still.

On my previous Nottingham visit, Notts County had gained promotion to Division One. Now they were in the more familiar position after a run of nine consecutive defeats (the worst record in their 149-year history) of battling against relegation. The good news that night, announced in The Five Ways, was of their 1-0 victory at Tranmere. They'd been outplayed, but Craig Westcarr had sneaked home a penalty, moving them out of the bottom four. I returned to number 85 Danethorpe Vale at 11.30pm with a slight spring in my step. Derrick had gone to bed, and Valerie was sitting in the living room in her dressing gown. For some reason I felt guilty.

This was the first time I had slept on Sherwood Estate in 48 years, a statistic of relevance or interest to absolutely no-one else.

As an avid newspaper reader, I decided that from each day's edition of the *Nottingham Post* (they'd recently dropped the word 'evening' possibly because the first edition was now on the streets soon after breakfast), I'd select a small quirky local item as a daily postscript, to appear at the end of each day's write-up (Sundays excepted of course). Here's the first:

THIS NOTTINGHAM

A competition has been launched to find Nottingham's best smile. Entrants need to send a photo plus a short story about their smile by April 29.

WEDNESDAY APRIL 20

OF BIKES AND THE BIRCH

I was born in The Firs Maternity Home, Mansfield Road, Sherwood. So, it transpired, was Valerie's sister, Gillian. The building was now a nursing home, and their mother had died there. In the midst of life etc...

On mornings such as these, I missed having a plan. Having plans was sensible, especially when writing a book. But my process tended to be more instinctive, to carry around with me the vague concept of the book, and respond to circumstances as and when they arrived. Or maybe the process was just more lazy. And in these early stages, when circumstances were still a bit thin on the ground, I was prone to a quiet inner panic, the fear there would be nothing to write about. I apologise for finishing that sentence on a preposition.

I got up at 6.30, somehow wrote for an hour, showered, then did forty minutes yoga. I always wanted to be a calm, cool, perfectly measured, laid-back person, hence the daily yoga. I was none of those things, nor did yoga quite remove my excitability and tendency to rush about too much, but it did dilute it. Doing yoga also rooted me in a place.

I liked my yoga sessions to smell nice. "Do you or Derrick mind me burning a joss stick in my room?" I asked Valerie.

"I don't, and Derrick won't even smell it," she replied.

Breakfast at number 85 was at 9am prompt. Valerie liked porridge with a sprinkle of sunflower seeds, and so did I, though their household bowls were half the size of my own. We three sat with our trays and passed the odd comment about the daytime television we were watching. I'd always considered daytime television the end of civilisation. Derrick and Valerie were both keen on

34

horse- racing and most weeks went to the local meeting at Southwell. I had no interest in the sport, outside an annual fiver on the Grand National.

Television had been in its infancy in my early Sherwood estate days. One spring Saturday in 1951 the family travelled five miles to Grandma Mortimer's house in Wollaton. She was the proud new owner of a nine-inch television set, and we peered through the grey fog of the postage-stamp-sized screen to witness Newcastle United win the first of their three FA Cups in five years. Since then, in more than sixty years, they've not had a sniff at any domestic trophy, which for many male and some female Geordies is life's greatest and least bearable tragedy.

Valerie and Derrick got together about eight years previously, and he'd upped sticks for the small journey from number 97. The interior of number 97 was for me already gaining a mythical status.

Valerie, and to a lesser extent Derrick, had impressively green fingers. As well as the arboreal delights of the front garden, the extensive back garden, which rose in sections, offered a small orchard, a mini-wood, an allotment, and a wee den under the apple tree where they put out grub to welcome the two foxes which were now regular visitors. As Nottingham Council sold off the Sherwood Estate gardens and allotments, Valerie bought extra lumps. Both she and Derrick dug and planted. Their current work included installing a new pond.

Part of me had always yearned to run soil through my fingers, and enjoy the creative delights of planting, digging and nurturing, while another part saw it all as pretty dull. In Tyneside, every terraced house I'd lived in had a front garden the size of a small mat, and to the rear, a back yard. Just occasionally I yearned to stretch out on a sun-lounger, or sniff a petunia.

In times of need, in times of alienation, I tended to buy a bike. I'd done it when living in the squalor of Shatila Palestinian Refugee Camp in Beirut, and now I was to do

35

it when living on Sherwood Estate. The bike, I sincerely believed, had the capability to save the planet if only we'd let it, just as the motor car had the capability to destroy the planet — and looked more than likely to do so. Not a day passed on Tyneside without bike usage, and I knew that my senses of place and peace of mind in Nottingham would both be stronger once I could get in the saddle.

The nearest bike shop was in Arnold, Sherwood's northern neighbour, two miles distant and always a slightly alien location in my youth. I jumped on a bus.

En route there was a sense of reassurance to see still in existence the small corner-shop barber, opposite Arnot Hill Park. This establishment once sold us lads a green glutinous goo. This gel, no doubt disastrously unhealthy for the follicles, set hair as rigid as concrete. Walk out in a Force 9 gale, and your DA or Tony Curtis would move not a millimetre. The fact that pulling a comb through your sacred locks produced in the comb's teeth the detritus of a sludge farm, worried us not a bit. Nor the fact it took four shampoos to get a lather. This was pre-shower days, you washed your hair in the sink, and the first few rinses left the water resembling the spillage round a leaking oil tanker.

My early adolescence was at the end of, and still influenced by, the Teddy Boy era, the first postwar youth counter-culture, and though Teds then outraged middle England, now they seem almost quaint. They did no illegal drugs, and when they fought, it was amongst themselves. I was too young to be a real Ted, the most infamous of whom in Nottingham was known as Big Bev. I once saw Big Bev walking up Parliament Street, purple draped jacket reaching his knees, drainpipe trousers like pipe cleaners and brothel creepers of hugely cartoonish size. His hair hung over his forehead like an oily bunch of black grapes. For all I know, nine-to-five, he was a wages clerk. Where is Big Bev now?

My new (or rather second-hand) black BSA mountain bike cost £50, or the equivalent of a meal out for two. Even as I pedalled away from the Arnold shop, my sense of security and well-being increased. Bikes are usually faster than cars in most of today's congested towns and cities, an advantage the industry's marketing people have failed to realise. Why not drop all that 'mountain bike' rubbish? Few of them ever encounter anything more mountainous than a tarmacked slope, and they should be rebranded with such names as *Urban Arrow* or *City Slicker*. Bikes also keep you in close contact with the sounds, the smells and the sheer physicality of your surroundings, something the sealed metal car is incapable of.

The Mortimer family moved to Arnold's northern extremity, Redhill, in 1963 as my father progressed up the social scale. For the time I worked for him, I alternated between a smart-suited salesman, driving round in a white-wall-tyre Ford Zodiac, wooing the draper shop old ladies (as they then seemed to me) to buy our stockings and lingerie, and returning to become a despatch clerk, parcelling up the same goods to send off at the local post office. This latter activity I did in the upstairs premises of Byron House, (the name being the nearest the Mortimer family came to poetry), a featureless piece of sixties architecture in Front Street, Arnold, which served as both stock room and office. My dad's firm was hardly a multi-national: comprising me, Pop, and sometimes a neighbour or cousin to do clerical work.

I cycled my new bike past Byron House and gazed up at the first-storey windows. It was now a solicitor's. What thoughts had gone through my head all those years ago, as I wrapped up the Pretty Polly nylons? Had I ever considered the larger picture, the years to come? Had I been happy, frustrated, bewildered, angry, philosophical, delusional?

My strategy, if strategy was not too strong a word, this early in my Nottingham stay, was to revisit as much past territory as possible, not for nostalgia reasons, but in the hope I would find a new context. Context was not something I had considered back then. Things happened, then other things.

Thus I also cycled round Arnot Hill Park, a relative outpost for us Sherwood lads. I'd never appreciated its beautiful lake busy with geese, ducks and swans, its herb garden, its aviary. The Park had a sense of landscaped arcadian splendour. Had anyone said that to me in 1959, I'd have thought them a prat. My mood was upbeat as I headed back along Mansfield Road, but changed to melancholic as I arrived at Valley Road Park, or 'the rec' as we called it. This long thin ribbon of a park stretching between two traffic islands along Valley Road at the bottom of the estate had been our nearest open space, and probably the most important place in our universe. We played football there. Climbed trees. Threw ourselves about on swings and roundabouts. Paddled in streams. And learnt about the opposite sex.

Though this was the Easter Holidays, the rec was now deserted. Two netless football goalpost structures stared blankly across a pitch at one another, the children's swings hung limply, and the slide was slightly tarnished through non-use. A great sadness descended on me, and I left the place swiftly.

The rec was our park, and our loyalty to it was fierce, albeit we knew it was seen as second-rate compared to Woodthorpe Park, which also faced the estate, across Mansfield Road on the eastern top side. Woodthorpe was a prosperous private area, an affluence which rubbed off on its park, ensuring that for us it never 'belonged' to Sherwood Estate in the way Valley Road Rec did.

Nor somehow did Sherwood Community Centre belong, despite physically being within the estate boundaries. It was on the edge, looking outwards across Mansfield Road, yet the fact you needed to walk out of the estate (even just a few yards) to gain entrance to the centre somehow created a barrier, and removed it from our everyday lives. Built in 1779, it was Sherwood's first building, and between 1851 and 1896 was owned by the Cartledge family, one of whose members I remembered opening the batting for Woodthorpe Cricket Club. The building was once owned by Sir Charles Seely, so all these years on I learned who my Sherwood Seely Primary School was named after. More of that school later.

The centre was also close to Elmswood Gardens, which ran down alongside Woodthorpe Park. Elmswood Gardens was solid and respectably middle-class, and it was here at the age of sixteen, by the large privet hedge of her parents' home, that I stole my first kiss from Sue Sanday, who was to cause my first relationship crisis.

Sue and I fell into one another with a natural warmth and attraction. What happened some months later might seem incredible to today's generation. Sue kept an account in her diary of our fairly innocent sexual behaviour. This somehow came into the possession of her father, a top cop in Nottingham. Faced with evidence of such depravity, the father immediately contacted my own parents, the upshot being Sue and I were banned from seeing one another, and made to feel

A hidden gem of Woodthorpe Park

ashamed of our natural loving responses. The ban lasted several months, during which time we had clandestine meetings in the grounds of Nottingham Castle and elsewhere. I had been brought up a Catholic (my mother was Catholic Irish and my father converted to Catholicism when he married), so I knew a bit already about lugging round sexual guilt. You carry that particular heavy suitcase lifelong.

When Sue and I eventually got back together, I never questioned the fact that we would soon get engaged, not long after marry, soon after have children, and all the rest. This was less to do with the unquenchable belief in the relationship's eternal love, more that these were the conventions everyone adhered to, and to question them would have shown an independence of mind I did not possess. Sue's dad was later transferred to run the Pannal Ash Police Training Academy at Harrogate, the family moved away, and this distance saw the relationship die a natural death, as slowly did my desire for and belief in marital domestic bliss.

A trip to the 1960s' slab that is Sherwood Library unearthed two recent reports on Sherwood Estate, 1996 and 2005, revealing that the estate was built to house ex-World War One veterans. I had never entered the library in my youth but would do so several times on my return.

Next to the library, Baguley's Funeral Directors was also a reminder of my early days, though its external sign was more a portent of the inevitability to come; *No Parking — Access Required 24 Hours.*

In the library I read that a foundation stone for the estate had been laid at 1 Danethorpe Vale, the street where I had lived for many years. Hundreds of time I had passed by this house yet never once noticed the stone. I vowed to seek it out. The library was on Mansfield Road, Sherwood's artery and the main thoroughfare from Nottingham going north. Unlike the estate, the Mansfield Road strip offered untold retail outlets. I counted a dozen take-aways, plus two delis, Polish, Turkish, Japanese,

40

Italian, Indian, French and Greek restaurants, and a couple of cut-price greasy joes into the bargain — a sense of the cosmopolitan nowhere evident back in the buttoned-up days of my adolescence.

At the top of Mansfield Road, one of the most distinctive buildings, the art deco Metropole Cinema, had been demolished. It closed in 1973 and first suffered the indignity of becoming a Kwik-Save supermarket before finally being put out of its misery. Built in 1937, the Metropole had been our regular Sunday night haunt. Neither the film itself nor the performance time was important. We'd enter the cinema at 7.30 and leave at 10pm to down a couple of swift pints before closing time in The Garden City, now a cavernous eating house, owned by the Hungry Horse chain. Often, entering the cinema mid-film, we'd see the second half of the main feature before the first. You got two films those days, and three different programmes a week. Outside the cinema would be a display of stills. If the photos included guns, these guns were obscured with a black strip, a token UK resistance against Hollywood's obsession with firearms.

In earlier years, The Metropole also offered the Saturday morning minors. Here, in one of the regular serials, I was terrified by one screen character with a club foot, recalled with dread apparently by many of my generation. These serials also offered an early example of how life could cheat on you. The final shot of one episode might see a character plunging to his or her death over a waterfall or cliff. The following week's opening shots would see the same character miraculously saved from said predicament. Loud boos would accompany such sleights of hand as we young bucks realised we had been manipulated. A favourite serial, *Flash Gordon*, included the villain Emperor Ming, a face of sculptured evil, and a character more real to me than virtually all flesh and blood people outside the cinema. Ming, incidentally, was played by by Charles Middleton, the first of three Middletons to feature in this book.

41

The regular Western shown as the main feature in the ABC Minors would have us emerge from the cinema in a state of high excitement to run down Danethorpe Vale furiously slapping our backsides, mimicking the horse-back cowboys.

We lads rarely came close to a horse, with the exception of the plodding hairy shire horses that pulled the drays of Shipstone's Brewery; we would occasionally stroke their large heads around which flies buzzed. This we did with a mix of fear and curiosity.

On the site of the Metropole cinema there now stood a Co-op supermarket of the distinctive shoe-box school of architecture. I turned away from the supermarket and made my way the few yards to 1 Danethorpe Vale, and the commemoration stone. Inset into the front of the house, which sat at a diagonal to the road junction and in a medium-sized garden, the half-obscured stone included the words (see over):

City of Nottingham Sherwood Housing Scheme. This stone was laid by the chairman of the Housing Committee Councillor Wm. Crane on the 22nd day of July, 1920.

The names of the Mayor, the Sheriff, and the assistant chairman were also included.

What ancient history this stone seemed to represent. Yet the year 1920 was fewer years removed from the time the Mortimer family moved onto the estate, than the year 2011 was from when we left it. I needed to calculate this several times to check the veracity, but it was true. You needed to walk up the path of number 1 to read the stone properly, so having come this far, I also knocked at the front door. It was eventually opened by a small elderly lady still half-hidden by the door frame. I had the distinct impression few people knocked on this door. In the friendliest manner I knew, I explained who I was, and what I was doing, and my interest in the foundation stone. I

42

The foundation stone at 1 Danethorpe Vale

learned the lady's name was Helen. I told her of my time living on Danethorpe Vale, and seeing her obvious nervousness, I dished up a whole series of geographical, historical and personal references about the estate to allay her possible fears that I was about to make a forced entry. In this I felt I was partially successful. A sudden rubbing round my legs was from her Jack Russell, Sky, who emerged from the house for a forage round the garden.

I chatted on Helen's doorstep for fifteen minutes. She seemed simultaneously pleased with the company, but unsure just how much to trust the same. Never once did I think of asking if I could come in. I did however say I would like to call for another chat if that was OK. There was more I wanted to know, yet did not want to overstay my welcome. Helen said, somewhat tentatively, that yes, it was alright if I called again, shut the door, and then I went away.

Valerie had mentioned a friend of hers, Ashley Turner, one year younger than me, who'd followed the same academic Nottingham path: Seely Primary, Haydn Road Junior, and High Pavement Grammar School. Ashley was a successful businessman with both a scooter shop for the disabled and a day nursery to his name. Like most Sherwood people who became entrepreneurs, he'd moved off the estate, but still lived close by in Albemarle Road, Woodthorpe. Having no alternative earth-shattering plans, I went to see him.

"I love that estate!" Ashley told me. "I've always loved it. I could never live far from it." Ashley's enthusiasm for Sherwood stretched to Nottingham overall — he was a season ticket holder for Notts County FC, Nottingham Forest, Notts County Cricket Club and Nottingham Panthers ice-hockey team. We both remembered seeing the legendary Canadian, Chic Zamick, play for the Panthers.

When he left High Pavement, Ashley worked for Lloyds Bank, on the same salary as I attracted in my first job — £6 a week. Though we hadn't known each other (one year's difference could be a big gulf) we bandied about the names of several familiar people: High Pavement teachers including The Three Smiths, Big Smith, Little Smith and Fat Smith the bullying PE teacher Coulson (were all PE teachers born sadists?) the Haydn Road Head, Ken 'Pop' Martin, whose jiggling Adam's apple fascinated me, and whose support for swimming saw Bulwell Baths named after him; the sympathetic head of High Pavement, 'Taff' Davies, with lips the size of inner tubes; and the assistant head, the gnarled and bitter 'Croc' Crosland, who instilled the fear of death into every pupil, feeding us his own brand of toxic racism as he banged his walking stick on the floor, his white moustache bristling with resentment.

Ashley most surprised me by producing, and lending me the book, *Bring Back the Birch*, the autobiography of Alan Birchenall, one of the magic Collin Green Sherwood trio who'd gone on to become professional footballers. The

44

book was ghost-written by Paul Mace, its awful title matched by the awful cover — a staged photo of Alan in mortar board and gown, brandishing a cane. This had more than a jokey reference for me and others of my generation. I was regularly caned and strapped at school by teachers, and even twice at home by my father.

Since becoming a father myself, the thought of such planned and clinical infliction of pain on your own child seemed beyond understanding. As for the school strap and canings, they created in me a deep hatred of the teachers involved, and a dark desire to do them wrong wherever possible.

Birchenall was a strong, muscular defender, who turned down an early offer to sign for Nottingham Forest due to his lifelong love of Notts County. This highly unusual piece of football romanticism always endeared him to me. He played for County, Chelsea, Crystal Palace, Sheffield United, and Leicester, and still works in the game as a PR man.

The second footballer, Mick Somers, was a tiny dot of a player, an incredibly tricky and talented winger, whose small stature prevented him reaching the highest peaks (excuse the pun) though he did play for Chelsea, Torquay and Hartlepool, the last team under Brian Clough and Peter Taylor. He now worked as a plumber.

Terry Bell was a cultured midfielder who played professionally for Portsmouth, present location unknown.

In his book Birchenall talks of growing up on the 'pristine' Sherwood Council Estate. There in the book was an evocative photo of the 1954 Haydn Road team and, beaming out, the fresh faces of Alan Birchenall and Mick Somers. No Terry Bell, but no Peter Mortimer either. There was a stage of my life when no greater tragedy seemed possible than my own failure to make the football grade, a failure accentuated by the success of the triumphant trio.

I played for various Nottingham clubs: Basford United, Sherwood Amateurs, Gedling Colliery, and, in the newly formed Sunday League (whose teams had less traditional names) Mercury FC. My giddiest heights were with Arnold St. Mary's, now Arnold Town, a semi-professional member of the then Midland League. To play for Arnold (even the reserves, which was my normal location) kept alive the fantasy that one day league soccer might become a reality.

It was, I told myself, only a matter of time before I followed in the footsteps of Messrs Bell, Birchenall and Somers. I'm now beginning to accept it might not happen.

THIS NOTTINGHAM

A drunken man accidentally set fire to his partner's front door while trying to kill a large spider with a makeshift flame thrower. Tony Kendrick was put on probation for a year and ordered to pay a total of £85 damages and costs.

THURSDAY APRIL 21

INFAMOUS EX-PUPILS,
BIRD DOG AND THE DEAD OAK

When I grew up on Danethorpe Vale, the front living room was barely in use; Christmas Day tea (when the family group would be large enough to require two sittings) and on other special occasions such as those canings, but otherwise the room sat empty, rows of tilted patterned plates staring silently from the three shelves of the polished Welsh dresser. For a short time my brother Alex and I were allowed a small billiard table therein — billiards still held sway over snooker in those days — and when our boxing careers were at their height (we were both school champions) Alex insisted we fought the heavyweight championship of the world in that room, fifteen three-minute rounds. He was two years older, and by round six had knocked me out, but dragged me to my feet to continue. This he did several times and for the last couple of rounds had to hold me up, before finally declaring himself global champ.

Half a century on, number 85 Danethorpe Vale's atti-tude to the front living room was similar to that of number 97 all those years ago. People rarely ventured in. Life overall here was lived mainly at the rear of the house; downstairs in the back living room and kitchen, while upstairs Valerie and Derrick's bedroom faced the back garden, leaving me as the sole and temporary repre-sentative of 'front of house living'. In my month's stay I only twice saw either of them enter the downstairs front room which was a dumping ground for either little-used utensils or objects whose future was still undecided. The room was basically a cupboard.

The sense of temporal displacement, that I was still trapped in a time lapse on the estate, was reinforced by

47

the daily sight of Kitty's Suzuki Jimny parked outside.

What was Sherwood Estate now? It was too pleasant to risk falling into the 'sink' category. And with an increasing number of properties sold into private hands, the word 'council' seemed to have been discreetly dropped. Significantly, there were now not only *For Sale* signs, but also signs saying *To Let.*

Before Thatcher's 1980 decision to put council houses on the market, council estates were immune from the house price obsession which overtook the UK. Council houses were where people lived, with no need to lose sleep over their market value. As properties came to be seen not only as where you lived but also as profit earners, this changed. The number of council properties now available for the public is greatly diminished as, like elsewhere, the 'market' dictates its own often harsh terms. And who builds new council houses any more?

Sherwood itself was never a fashionable part of Nottingham in my youth, but now seemed to be on the up. A monthly street market had just been established, June saw both a Sherwood Festival and a Sherwood Arts Week, and the Mansfield Road area boasted a good few examples of public psychedelia to warm the cockles of this old hippy's heart. More of them later.

Ashley had given me the news that the High Pavement Grammar School premises in Bestwood (it later became a Sixth Form College) had been demolished. The loss felt personal. I first attended High Pavement in 1956, spending the initial year in the old Victorian site in Stanley Street, Hyson Green, before being part of the initial intake of pupils in the brand new Bestwood building, which was perched on a hill top looking south across the playing fields towards Sherwood and the city centre.

If the site had been impressive, the building was less so, a precursor to much of the tatty 1960s' architecture. How ironic it had now been knocked down, while the ancient building it replaced was still going strong.

Not that I much enjoyed the High Pavement experience. Most of my mates failed the 11-plus and attended Claremont Secondary School on Hucknall Road. They left school at the age of fifteen to take up apprenticeships in joinery, plastering or plumbing, or to work in one of the big Nottingham factories such as Players, Boots or Raleigh.

They were bringing home real wage packets while I was sweating for A-levels, absorbing great chunks of Goethe and living on the pathetic money from my week-end grocery delivery round at the Hucknall Road Co-op. I wanted out of school. I wanted to be part of the real world, like them.

And much of school *was* useless, though later I was appreciative of taking A-level French and German, which left me as one of that small British minority who were not totally monoglot. When I become the UK dictator,

Public psychedelia in Sherwood

learning at least one foreign language for the entire population will be among my first dictats.

I cycled that morning from Sherwood Estate up to the school site in Bestwood, a mile-and-a-half route I walked twice daily as a pupil, often with a Park Drive cupped secretly in my hand in case a teacher should drive or cycle past. Where once had been the school and playing fields was now a private estate. The smaller houses were at the bottom, the larger with the splendid views at the top. So strong was my image of this hilltop school, this distinctive landmark in which I studied for six years, that I was unable to take in the fact it no longer existed. I was convinced I had only to close my eyes for two seconds and on re-opening them, all would be as it once had been, this new housing estate banished from view.

The private estate streets were named after ex-High Pavement School people, a fact of which many of the residents were probably ignorant. Thus there was Millige Close — Fred Millige was our sixth form French teacher who would secretly slip us a John Player cigarette during seminars on Victor Hugo or Rimbaud in the small stockroom. Also Crosland Close, after the aforementioned tyrant and assistant head and Jackson Close — the maths teacher with the ill-fitting top dentures which moved of their own volition. At one stage Jackson was brought in by my father for my private tuition, to redress my poor maths performance at school. Pavior Close referred both to the collective name for ex-pupils (Old Paviors), also to Pete Pavior, one time head-boy, a sporting luminary, an indecently talented individual you one day expected to rule the planet. He later became my parents' GP.

Davies Close — the one-time 'Satchmo' head teacher Taff Davies; Gilbert Close — the ancient and sticklike English teacher Mr Gilbert (first name unknown) on whom I swear they based Chalky from the Bash Street kids; Blackburn Close — the chubby woodwork teacher with desirable daughter Linda; plus other names such as

50

Slater and Murray which were vaguely familiar yet whose identity I could not specifically recall.

Two of the best known names from High Pavement Grammar School were missing. My late English teacher Stanley Middleton (the second Middleton in the book), who became a Booker-Prize-winning novelist, and whose influence on me was to prove seminal. More about Stanley later. The second name was even better-known. Yet this was an old pupil unlikely to have a street named after him, nor be featured in any school roll of honour, nor ever be mentioned in despatches from High Pavement Grammar School. That person's name was Harold Shipman.

It was not long before I was again plunged into melancholia, and again at the same location as the previous day, Valley Road Park, the rec. Days and weeks long had been spent on this thin ribbon of park. Entire holidays would pass here; in the evenings and week-ends we would charge from Danethorpe Vale over Valley Road clutching the freshly dubbined football. Or we would mess about hours long on the swings, the roundabout, the slide. When slightly older we ran yelling through the two underground tunnels of the Day Brook which bordered one edge of the park, our shouts echoing off the walls. These tunnels were now secured against such access.

The other side of the Day Brook, now built up with houses, had been a small woodland, where a girl who I will call Jane Bryant afforded me my first sexual experience as I and several other curious but uncertain young males fumbled about with her nether regions while she chewed gum and looked vacant. I had little idea what a vagina was or looked like, or what you were supposed to do with it. The others were in a similar state of ignorance so we poked about a bit, then went home.

Sex education with family or school was virtually non-existent. Had my mother or father sat me down to explain it, I'm not sure who would have died of embarrassment first. My only relevant sexual reference from the school establishment was the High Pavement head gathering together us pubescent males one morning to announce, "I am now going to say a word that will shock you all — masturbation."

We were all duly shocked. The head went on to explain that we were at an age where we felt the need to indulge this habit, but to long continue such an evil activity — for evil was surely was what it was — was wicked and must be resisted at all costs. Soon enough, he assured us, the desire would pass away. Naturally it didn't. It raged like a forest fire, yet whenever I 'indulged' such 'self-abuse' I was left wracked with guilt. I sought ways of gaining satisfaction without using my hands, arguing this then would not really 'count.' I rubbed up against a variety of hard surfaces when no-one was looking, a method I thought might partially offset the sense of shame, yet such was the power of the head's dire warnings that pleasuring myself — even in this unconventional fashion — regularly left me looking to the heavens for the avenging thunderbolt which would strike me down.

Another landmark of the rec was a great oak tree — now a dead 15ft stump — beneath which we would gather and where on a portable record player I first heard the sounds of Elvis's *Hound Dog* and the Everly Brothers' *Bird Dog*. None of us had ever heard sounds like this, the onset of music that was to sweep away an entire culture and radically change our lives.

The rec's football pitch, with its two slightly wonky junior size sets of goalposts, lacked any footballers, just as the park itself lacked any people. The children's rides were corralled inside a safety-conscious wood-shavings square surface. But there were no children.

And some things were turned on their heads. Where the open grassland would at that time have been loud with the shouts of footballers, now it was silent. Where, beyond the railings, Valley Road would have been mainly silent and deserted, now it was thunderous with traffic. At one time a ball kicked over the railings would bob about on the road till retrieved. Had a ball now been kicked over it would have been burst within seconds under the non-stop conveyor belt of wheels.

All the above induced the aforementioned melancholia, which I carried back to the house with me. Valerie had cooked a meal of pork chops, potatoes, cabbage, carrots and gravy, grub which itself seemed to suggest another age. Along with her own cheery manner, the tasty food partly offset my low feelings, and indeed she and Derrick had better things to do than listen to my whingeing. Despite Derrick's retirement, he'd been called out to do a day's roofing. At such times Valerie always worried for his safety. Did roofers not wear safety harnesses? "No," said Derrick in a tone to suggest such attire might be seen in the trade as girly to say the least. When I'd worked in the North Sea with fishermen, they showed a similar resistance to safety lines, and hence lots of them drowned. Not wanting to appear soft, I'd not worn one either.

Derrick and Valerie's house was pretty low-tech, even for such a man as myself, immune to many of the charms of high technology. There was no answer phone, no satellite TV, no sign of a computer (though a small model, rarely used, did put in a later appearance) no emails, no texts, no Twitter or Facebook. The phone was the old-fashioned non-peripatetic variety, so all conversations took place in the echoey downstairs hall. None of this bothered me.

That day there was to be no escaping the melancholia, for it paid another visit during my time in the Five Ways in the evening. Until recently the distinctively panelled walls of this pub had been hung with dozens of portraits by local artist Ken Yarwood. One of the pub's bars was named after Yarwood, who was now dead. The drawings were of the Five Ways regulars. They had recently been taken down and locked away. I never saw these works of art, yet still found myself missing them and wanting them replaced, as if somehow their presence symbolised the individuality of an English pub.

As I walked through The Five Ways door, the record playing was The Shirelles' *Will You Love Me Tomorrow?*, whose evocation of the early 60s was almost all-consuming. Hearing it was counter-productive to my attempts to view my Nottingham stay through a contemporary lens. There was a pool match in the Sherwood Room, members of the local bird club were meeting in the Ken Yarwood Room, while the Concert Room hosted a wedding reception. A group of the wedding guests emerged into the corridor bar. They were young, the men mostly shaven-headed, often tattooed, dressed in trackie bottoms, jeans, t-shirts, hoodies and trainers, so I assumed the wedding invitation had included the phrase 'Dress Optional'.

They hung about in the corridor, with the occasional monosyllabic utterance. They fed the fruit machine, stabbed at their mobiles, and if they looked at me, I looked away. One of the young men was up before the magistrate in a few days' time, and there was chat as to whether he'd get six or eighteen months.

A small incident this first night coloured what followed. I sat at the bar, making a few general notes in the small notebook in which I regularly scribbled. The barman, a heavily tattooed man called John with a distinctive face that suggested a Goya cartoon, had already cast some strange looks and eventually he came over, and in the broadest Nottingham accent, said, "Yo from the child support agency or summat? Yo mekking me paranoid, wi' that notebook o' yorn." I spluttered something ridiculous about being a writer and put the book away, as if in appeasement. It cut little ice. "Mekking me bleddy paranoid," he said and walked away. For the next hour he'd cast me the occasional suspicious glance, despite the non-appearance of the notebook. I did speak to John on several other occasions that night, but those initial sentences were by far the longest I heard from him. From thereon replies were mainly monosyllabic.

54

John's accusatory glances, his suspicions I was a state investigator, plus the edgy presence of the wedding guests made for a less than totally relaxed spell at the bar. I walked home from my erstwhile local without total peace of mind.

THIS NOTTINGHAM

A one-legged driver was given a parking ticket when he pulled over — because his false leg fell off. Lee Scarrott of Clifton received a £70 fine after a five minute emergency stop in St. Peter's Gate, Nottingham.

FRIDAY APRIL 22

LATIN MASS AND FOOTBALL CHANTS

It was Good Friday, though the adjective 'bad' probably better sums up the start of the day at number 85, Danethorpe Vale. The washing machine repair man called and after fifteen minutes of his expert labour, the kitchen was flooded with water, the machine pronounced as useless, and he was presenting Valerie with a bill for £25. Valerie and Derrick responded to these traumas with a remarkable stoicism.

I went up to my room to stare at the wardrobe. This was oak, dark-stained, with a distinctive mirror whose design suggested Arabic influence. The wardrobe, like all old wardrobes, looked sturdy enough to withstand collision with a juggernaut.

I had not owned a wardrobe in twenty-five years. Much of my life, post-Sherwood Estate had consisted in the casting off of wardrobes. Being wardrobe-free, like pushing your bed against the wall as opposed to centre-room, symbolised liberation, a rejection of stifling conformity. This liberation had not happened immediately. As I moved several times, the wardrobes slowly got smaller until one day I awoke with that startling moment of epiphany, "I do not need a wardrobe at all!" Thus a new chapter of my life began.

Today was the big local derby in the championship, Nottingham Forest v Leicester City, both teams still with a chance of making the play-offs.

I supported the less fashionable Notts County, and unless County were actually playing Forest, a fairly rare occurrence as Forest usually occupied a higher division, I would as soon contemplate visiting Forest's City Ground as I would jumping down a volcano.

Yet once you leave your native city, you become less tribal, more expansive in your appreciation of it, and in the face of taunts from Scouses, Geordies, Cockneys or Brummies (for all of whom Notts County were a lower division irrelevance) my defence of Nottingham football culture required the evidence of Forest's glories to have any substance. Thus I began to view Forest with less hostility, and with the glory years of Brian Clough I realised I had even acquired some kind of emotional attachment.

Living on Tyneside, and witnessing the locals' scathing sense of all things connected with the Mackems (Sunderland folk) reminds me just how strong parochial tribalism can be. Part of me envies it, another part now finds it ridiculous.

This was my first trip into the city centre on this visit. I walked up through the estate and caught a bus from Mansfield Road. The bus has become the transport of the poor and the old, and, nationwide, bus services have withered away just at the time they should have had heavy investment. Nottingham's splendid hub system partially bucked the trend.

The vast proportion of the population who never catch a bus miss several delights, especially on the double-decker, especially upstairs on the front seat, a much sought-after vantage point for those in the know. This seat offers both a panoramic view of the world spread out before you, but also an almost dreamlike giddy sense of moving through impossibly narrow spaces. The vehicle wobbles its way round corners, negotiates tiny gaps in the traffic. No train, nor car, nor any other form of transport can match this upstairs front-seat experience, and it costs no more than the normal ticket, which for me, given the national subsidy of bus fares for senior citizens, was nowt.

Nottingham's city centre can boast The Market Square (Slab Square to the cognoscenti) which few cities can rival, dominated at one end by the imposing Grecian pillared grandeur of The Council House (as one wag put it, "If that's a Nottingham council house, what do the private properties look like?").

The two stone lions at each side of the Council House have always been a favourite meeting point, and are said to roar if a virgin passes by. No sound has ever been heard.

The square, whose sense of wide open space seems to lift the human spirit, had been freshly resurfaced, and on this beautiful spring day was criss-crossed by hundreds of walkers. Hung on the Council House frontage to mark the coming St. George's Day was a giant St. George's flag — further attempts to rescue our flag from far right loonies and football boot-boys. Two o'clock, and the sonorous booms of Little John, said to be the loudest chiming clock in the country after Big Ben, rang out across the square. Warning — if you have false teeth, Little John will make them rattle. On a good day you could hear the chimes in Sherwood.

One innovation in the square were the new fountains, for once actually *designed* for people's participation, so that dozens of bathing-suited kids ran and squealed their delight through the perfectly safe water features, bringing the kind of celebratory innocence modern UK city centres, blighted by the malevolence of binge drinking, much need.

This was the start of the Easter holidays, adding to the sense of release and festivity. I walked from the centre to Trent Bridge, through Arkwright Street and The Meadows area, rebuilt and unrecognisable from my youth.

The grass-covered banks of the Trent, viewed from Trent Bridge, resembled some giant poppy field as hundreds of red-shirted Forest fans stretched out in the sunlight.

The River Trent may lack the iconic quality of the Tyne, the Mersey or the Clyde, and has no songs to match the anthems of *Ferry Across the Mersey* or *Fog on the Tyne*. Nottingham is an inland city, which in many cultural and commercial ways dilutes the importance of its river. But consider this; within a stone's throw of this bridge can be found the grounds of Nottingham Forest FC (chosen as a Euro 96 venue) Notts County FC, the inter-national test ground of Notts County Cricket Club, and the Holme Pierrepoint National Water Sports Centre, an important focal pint for the 2012 Olympics.

As regards the two football grounds, it's said that County's is in the city, and Forest's in the county. The Trent is the city boundary and the grounds stare across at one another over the water. There was a large crowd of almost 30,000 for the local derby. Forest used to run out to the sounds of *Robin Hood*, the slightly cheesy song from the Richard Greene TV series. Now it was Prokofiev's *Romeo & Juliet*, just like Sunderland FC, just like *The Apprentice*. This was followed — for reasons I didn't understand except perhaps the fact their then manager Billy Davies was a Scot — by *Mull of Kintyre*, a song which was either among the most stirring ever heard, or 100 per cent naffdom — I could never decide.

Certainly, with the crowd in full voice accompaniment, it was an emotionally charged preparation for the game.

The match was mainly undistinguished, the suspicion was that neither team was likely to be playing the top league in the next season. In the final seconds the Leicester goalie Chris Wale let a weak shot slide through his fingers, the kind of non-save to make even a Sunday league keeper blush. This gave Forest the three points.

A word here about football's most unsung and curious fraternity, a group of men who attend the match, are given vantage point positions superior to any spectator, yet never get to see a single second of the action. I write of those stewards, clad in bright orange or yellow coats who spend the entire 90 minutes squatting on their little seats pitchside, backs to the game, meticulously studying the crowd for signs of errant behaviour. Such men have an iron discipline. I tried to think of a distraction which might cause them to turn and view the game. Certainly not a goal, for this is when they were at their most intent in examining the crowd, their studied seriousness in greatest contrast to the wild celebrations of those they

59

were surveying. What *would* make them turn towards the pitch? Possibly the parachuting into the centre circle of Godzilla, or a machine-gun-spraying maniac running amok? And then I remembered; a streaker always did the trick.

Post-match I walked back to the city centre. Were I a painter, I would capture Trent Bridge seen from the riverside after a Forest game; a Lowry-style vision, a solid, unbroken trudge of figures silhouetted against the sky, thousands of people packed for two hundred yards onto a narrow conveyor belt that seemed to carry them across the river of its own volition.

A few louts roared and bellowed their way up Arkwright Street, and the city centre was beginning to liven up for the evening, a time of day when most people over the age of 25 became conspicuously absent. I sat in the square, and stared at the ugly ten-storey Pearl Assurance building opposite. Besotted, as all kids were, with Americana, I'd been thrilled when the square boasted its own mini-skyscraper and was eager for more of the same, totally unaware how ill-fitting such architecture was to the aesthetics of a centre where some of the historic buildings were half-timbered. Luckily only one more high-rise building had been allowed, a slightly less offensive edifice, imaginatively lit at night.

Yates' Wine Bar (which added an ungrammatical 's' after Yates' to its sign) had been a favourite city centre watering hole for us young bloods. It now boasted a red carpet to welcome drinkers, at the top end of which stood two burly bouncers. But it still sold its strong Australian white wine; two glasses of the same were reputed to bring most Nottingham lasses to a state of sexual abandon, a claim never substantiated in my experience.

Live violinists had been one of Yates' distinctions. The fiddles of yesteryear had given way to loud, discordant music, and the toilets were tatty. Yates' glory days seemed behind it. Today was the Wetherspoons generation. Opposite Yates is the historic Bell Inn, a music-free

60

warren of small rooms and alleyways, where the human race seemed a different, less aggressive species than the one fuelled on flashing lights and high decibels. I'd once featured the pub in the first mawkish attempt at a novel, a piece of writing which happily remains unpublished.

If I stood still and silent for a few moments back here in Nottingham, a tug would invariably pull me in a certain direction. This method was successful various times and on this day the tug pulled me towards the Vale, the third regular drinking hole of my Sherwood Estate days, a handsome art deco building, and one of the few pubs where you could walk round the entire perimeter unobstructed, though the urge to do so probably indicated a sad life.

The Vale was at the junction of Mansfield Road and Thackeray's Lane, just beyond the estate's Eastern tip; its interior was beautifully panelled, the ornate doors with distinctive wide brass strips for handles, a sense of slightly faded elegance which imbued a certain soporific atmosphere. Whenever I drank in The Vale, I felt older than my years.

The pub was close to the Church of the Good Shepherd where in early days brother Alex and I were sent to both mass and Sunday school. At the former I was fascinated by the small puffs of incense smoke left by the swinging chalice, fascinated by the beautiful, if incomprehensible, language of the Latin service and the ornate garb of the priest. I hardly gave God a second thought. Sunday school was pure tedium, as a shrivelled-up prune of a woman whose lack of human warmth or celebration suggested she had died years previously, prattled on about the scriptures, while brother Alex and I dreamed of lighting fires, building dams or pulling the legs off spiders.

The Catholic hold over the family weakened with the passing of the years. My father, I've mentioned, converted when he married my mother, who had emigrated to England from County Cavan to work as a nurse, but his conversion was always token, and he had little interest in the rural Irish culture of my mother's upbringing. In summer, my mother regularly took her sons back to her small village of Butler's Bridge, though our father rarely came with us. Slowly these visits decreased, then stopped altogether. It was some years later I made the pilgrimage to rediscover my Irish links. I'd abandoned the faith years before, though Catholicism never truly goes away, and throughout life was always lurking somewhere in the shadows.

Only a small percentage of customers in The Vale that Friday night were bladdered, though when I emerged, a hopelessly drunk young man the other side of Mansfield Road was roaring across the road, "You f*****g whore! You f*****g c**t!", the object of his attention being a young woman with whom he'd obviously had an altercation.

The man eventually staggered off into the night, still occasionally bellowing, this time to no-one, and the woman made off the other way, looking hunched and desolate. By my age, the darker side of human nature shouldn't really have upset me so, but it still did..

THIS NOTTINGHAM

Forty-five years on, veteran pop stars The Monkees will play at The Royal Concert Hall, Nottingham on May 25, tickets £32.50–£100. Singer Davy Jones commented, "I tell some good Robin Hood jokes."

SATURDAY APRIL 23

ENGLAND AND ST GEORGE

St. George's Day, and I slept in. By the time I emerged, Derrick was watching horseracing on the telly and studying the list of runners in the *Daily Mail*. He and Valerie regularly attended the meetings at nearby Southwell. As kids, my brother Alex and I would occasionally be taken to the point-to-point meetings at Cropwell Bishop, though horse folk to me always seemed a race apart, if you'll excuse the pun.

My mother's words of wisdom included the phrase, "I've never met a poor bookie," in contrast to which she'd point to the succession of impoverished wretches with frayed collars and sallow skin emerging from the local bookmaker's premises. For Valerie and Derrick, racing was just the odd small flutter.

Among the city's most famous people historically was The Sheriff of Nottingham, generally seen as a bad egg when portrayed on screen by the likes of Alan Rickman. The main ambition of the Sheriff was the thwarting and elimination of the heroic Robin Hood, for which he received the opprobrium of the viewing public.

I'd never met the contemporary Sheriff while living in Nottingham, but on this morning she (yes, I know our expectations were for a male) was just across Valley Road officially opening the new *pétanque* or *boules* courts. I said hello to Councillor Penny Briggs. And she said hello back. There's not much more to report except there are still twenty Sheriffs in the UK (though none as famous as Nottingham) and the phrase Sheriff of Nottingham does not conjure up a slightly fragrant well-dressed female, but such a specimen Penny Briggs was.

Nottingham had arranged St George's Day celebrations in the city centre. The English ambivalence towards their own identity was perfectly captured via St George, whose day usually passed without remark, whose history and relevance were virtually unknown to most, and whose flag had mainly negative associations.

Some attempts had been made in Nottingham to redress this. On a beautifully sunny Saturday, the Market Square was thronged with people. Kids could have their photo taken with an amiable dragon (presumably killed by George later), there was a traditional mummers' play, brass band music and rows of stalls.

Whenever or wherever I mingled in crowds — at least from the North Midlands up — I was struck by how strongly the native accent survived. Despite our becoming a global village, despite being exposed to multi-national cultural influences, and non-stop exposure to the mass media, regional accents remained stubbornly healthy, and more than 90 per cent of people I encountered in Nottingham, black or white, young or old, spoke in that flattened East Midlands throwaway style which so much helped to define the area's character and culture.

Nor, despite pessimists' views on the homogenisation of our city centres via the proliferation of chain stores and identikit shopping centres, was there any way you could mistake the centre of Nottingham for that of Sheffield, Manchester, Liverpool or any other of our main conurbations, all of which remained stubbornly individual.

The sun beat down, and the day's serious drinkers were already about their business, many bedecked in flags or other red and white paraphernalia. Outside The Bell, the *al fresco* drinkers were corralled into a pen. Occasionally one would drift out, only to be herded back in by the attendant stewards who took on the duties of sheepdogs. It was a long time since I had spent several continuous hours in this city centre. Nor had I realised the historical clout of its hostelries. Yates' Wine Lodge proudly proclaimed on its exterior that it had originated as Talbots in 1686. This was only two years earlier than the nearby and distinctly named The Royal Children, whereas The Bell itself dated back to 1437.

These statistics were impressive enough till you walked round the corner and came to The Salutation, rumoured by some to be in danger of closing, whose pedigree dates back to 1240.

Few cities could match such an historic cluster of pubs in such a small area, and this was before we considered the granddaddy of them all, the one and only Trip to Jerusalem, which at 1198 was the oldest pub in the country, partially built into the rock beneath Nottingham Castle. Hewn from Sherwood sandstone, the bar's ceiling was said occasionally to drop a sandy deposit on the top of your pint. Elsewhere the pub was a low-beamed warren of small rooms which somehow survived without a five yearly make-over by interior designers.

The Trip had been a resting place for those *en route* to the Crusades, and as I emerged to walk up to Nottingham Castle, there before me, on a giant white steed, clip-clopping over the cobbles was a fully-fitted out crusader (or St George himself?). There was something startling about this medieval manifestation in a busy modern city centre street. The large horse was draped in red and white flags, as was the rider, complete with chain mail. He also carried aloft a giant St George's flag. Man and horse clip-clopped their way past the crowds sun-bathing on the grass by Robin Hood's statue outside the Castle. This being Nottingham, the crowds included a good few Muslims. I wondered what they made of it all.

The statue, cast in bronze by sculptor Phillip Clay in 1949, is a tourist focal point. In its early days Robin's arrow was regularly stolen by Saturday night party-goers and was now welded on. The same sculptor had made a series of bronze plaques on the castle wall behind. These showed Robin in various situations, including kneeling at the altar with Maid Marian (well-known Nottingham joke: "Who's Maid Marian? — Most of the Merry Men.") Curiously, a quiver of bows was still on Robin's back, rather like a joiner turning up for his matrimonials lugging his tool kit.

65

All the historical pubs overflowed. In The Royal Children was a two-piece band called *Mix Tape*, whose drummer wore a gorilla mask, possibly sponsored by Cadbury. A group of middle-aged men from Long Eaton, dressed like The Blues Brothers, staggered in and told me they'd celebrated St George's Day this way for ten years. Their women followed them in. One sang a song loudly, then fell asleep. The group were all drunk, but not aggressively so.

Back to Danethorpe Vale for Valerie's meal of sausage, egg, chips, beans, tea, and bread and butter. Such fodder was unsung by celebrity chefs and food writers, but secretly adored by millions. Also secretly adored, for a man who normally cooked for himself, was the fact I could just turn up at number 85 and tuck in. I paid Valerie £70 a week for the room, which included breakfast, and for every evening meal I gave her a fiver. This suited both parties.

Several times Derrick Junior had come to the front door, exchanged a few brief words with his father, often with raised voices, then gone. I was keen to secure my entrance to my childhood home at number 97, but always missed the elusive son.

"Why not invite him in?" I asked Derrick Senior, but he shook his head. All families had their individual quirks and rituals, and this was no exception. Derrick Junior called daily at number 85, but did not cross the threshold. Nor had Derrick Senior and Valerie crossed the threshold of number 97 (six doors down) for several years.

"I need to talk to him," I said, "I need to get into that house."

"Not sure 'ow yo'll do that," said Derrick Senior.

"I have to," I said, "it's the house of my childhood."

"Wa'll 'av ter see," said Derrick.

I sensed things had never been easy between father and son, and that maybe I was out of my depth. After 48 years I was within shouting distance of the house in which I'd grown up, a house soaked through with memory

66

and association. Six times now I had walked along the street to stare at the dilapidated exterior, not once daring to venture through the gate onto the path overgrown with weeds and long grass. A strange emotional and psychological battle raged inside me about this house, and it would be another two weeks before I could make sense of it, or find resolution.

Meantime I cycled to Hucknall Road Co-op and bought some Easter eggs. The shop offered four for the price of three, and when I handed them over back on Danethorpe Vale, Valerie said, "wa could give the extra one to young Derrick" a splendid suggestion which hinted she was supporting my efforts. Soon afterwards I learned Derrick Junior had taken the egg and gone.

Though I drank considerably less alcohol than yesteryear, my love of pubs had grown, less as places to get bladdered in, more as necessary social centres for our increasingly fragmented communities. It was this same spirit of sociability that saw me invite Derrick and Valerie that night to the Five Ways. Being Easter Saturday I expected a crowded pub, but it was virtually empty, the main concert room closed, one table of four people in the Sherwood Room, and a handful of folk in the small bar.

The pub had booked two separate 'artistes' that night; 'Down Memory Lane with Johnnie Evans', plus a female singer called P'zazz. "Yo'd probably like Johnnie Evans," the landlady Yvette said to me. I tried not to take this as a personal affront as I watched the ageing singer go through his saccharine numbers from Engelbert Humperdink *et al*. With some alarm I realised she probably saw me as an old gadgie.

Johnnie was performing in the intimacy of the bar to the scattered few. He had the kind of unexceptional voice you might hear up a window cleaner's ladder. "Probably earns a few bob to help him aht in 'is retirement," said Valerie. After three songs, members of one table got up and left. But where was P'zazz?

67

"She couldn't mek it," said landlord Steve, "'Er windscreen wipers broke."

Was there a clause in the contract about such an eventuality, I wondered?

This was the last time I ever saw Steve or his wife.

At home, Derrick was usually amiable, but in The Five Ways he seemed withdrawn, possibly to do with the Derrick Junior business, or the fact the couple rarely visited pubs. He surprised me at one stage by saying, "Valerie stood me up 'ere once, I waited half an hour, then went 'om."

What happened?

"Just forgot," she answered and laughed, a moment's welcome antidote to a strangely muted hour in The Five Ways, which on reflection was the real start of my falling out of love with a venue that had once been so close to my heart.

If there was some small cause for celebration it was Notts County's 2–1 away win at Swindon, all but banishing fears of relegation. Forest's late surge has put them in a favourable position for the play-offs. These changes of fortune, I told myself in self-congratulatory manner, had come about since my own arrival back in Nottingham.

THIS NOTTINGHAM

People with George or Georgina as their first name are offered a free pint at the Grosvenor pub, Mansfield Road to mark St George's Day.

SUNDAY APRIL 24

THE SUNDAY OUTINGS
OF YESTERYEAR

I awoke in a tired listless, pessimistic state, close to indulging that most debilitating of emotions, self-pity. I seemed unable to stir myself, convinced this estate no longer had any relevance for me. I had been away too long, the journey had been too far. How naïve to believe I could return and make a connection. There was no connection, and I was a stranger in a strange land.

To cheer myself up, I glanced at the list of activity groups in Sherwood Community Centre's programme. From the top then: Alcoholics Anonymous, Alzheimers, Aphasia, Carers' Support, Coping With Anxiety... I put the programme down. Too much fun was bad for you.

No matter. The country always had the Royal Wedding to look forward to. I'd been living on this estate for the first major royal celebration during my life, the 1952 coronation. Our national mood was much different then. Deferential forelock-tugging to the higher orders had all but disappeared now, partly through a refreshing mistrust of our 'superiors', partly because a lot of people simply didn't like anybody.

To prepare myself for Sherwood Estate, I'd gathered together a small collection of books focussing on life in, and the history of, council estates. The longer I was here, the less inclined I was to open any of them. I'd also watched the TV documentary, *The Great Estate* written and presented by the author Michael Collins, and directed by Chris Wilson.

Collins had grown up on Haygate Estate, South London, and took us through the history since the first example, The Boundary Estate, which opened in Shoreditch in 1900. The idea of rehousing the less well-off of the working class, many of whom lived in abject poverty, was mooted in the Royal Commission set up by Lord Salisbury in 1883, but it was the seething sense of agitation post-World War One that led to the first major legislation, Lloyd George's revolutionary 1919 Housing and Town Planning Act.

By 1970 one third of the population was living in council housing, but exactly ten years later in 1980, a radical reversion of policy came in the shape of Margaret Thatcher's 'Right to Buy' legislation. Ironically many estates since that time had declined, and earned themselves the description 'sink'. This was not true of Sherwood, which seemed quiet and generally well-maintained. The latest survey showed 1337 households with 3,400 people. No-one built council houses anymore, and your chance of getting one was remote. Thatcher's Right to Buy policy, trumpeted as a great egalitarian move, paid homage to the British obsession with houses as money-making opportunities, an obsession at the root of virtually all the ills that have befallen the housing market since, and one that has put the majority of housing beyond the grasp of the majority of people. As soon as we were brainwashed into seeing houses as cash cows, we were lost. They are places to live in. We complain if prices for cabbages, cars, washing machines or summer holidays go up. Why on earth do we cheer when the same applies to house prices?

The policy has also left one-time council estates as an ill-defined social area, a strange cocktail of the public and the private. Though I'm also wary of some modern middle-class historians pointing to a golden age, and the one-time pride felt by people living on council estates. I never felt this pride when growing up in Sherwood, and, like many others was reluctant to reveal my home location when trying to come on to a female at the Palais de Dance or Locarno in the city centre. The young women were more impressed with well-off lads from West Bridgford or Woodthorpe. For many, the estates could be a trap, and breaking free was seen as an achievement.

Derrick and Valerie, as if tapping into my sense of *ennui*, announced they were taking me out for Sunday dinner. I assumed this would be up the road in Sherwood, but it was a fifty-mile round trip to a fish and chip shop in Matlock Bath. Both were drivers, but rarely used the old VW, which sat parked outside the house. There were no garages on the estate. This day Valerie drove, and like most male partners, Derrick offered regular advice, which, being an excellent driver, Valerie didn't need.

Much of Nottingham's surrounding countryside was tame compared to the North-East, and without that sense of wilderness you experienced in the hills of Northumberland. Large centres of population were always close at hand in the East Midlands. Having said that, Matlock Bath was a striking location, a small spa town developed Swiss-style in the Victorian era. The town ran alongside the River Derwent, and unusually for this region, sat in a deep wooded gorge. One distinctive feature was the cable cars which spanned high over the narrow town like decorative lanterns, slowly carrying visitors up to and away from the lofty vantage points.

Thousands flocked here for Easter Sunday, giving the sense of Bank Holidays from another era. Matlock Bath was a magnet for bikers, serried ranks of their powerful machines lining the streets, their large fuel tanks like gorged insects. Motorbikers had once been young tearaways in the manner of the Brando film *The Wild Ones*. Today, the high cost of the machines meant bikers were more likely to be middle-aged and respectable, their swelling bellies bulging out of the tight leathers which were still *de rigueur*.

This sense, while being back in Nottingham, of going on an old-fashioned Bank Holiday drive to an old-fashioned town, travelling in the back seat of the car, via non-motorway roads, brought the bizarre sensation that Derrick and Valerie, despite being roughly my contemporaries, were at this moment my mum and dad.

71

On the return journey, the giant portion of fish and chips, followed by a large cone of ice-cream, sat in my stomach like setting concrete, and once back home, I jumped straight on the bike in an attempt to minimise the solidifying effects.

We'd driven close to the home of one of my former football clubs, Basford United of the Notts Alliance. From studying the league tables in the *Nottingham Post*, I knew the club still existed, and cycled off a few miles in search of the Mill Street ground where once I'd paraded my skills. But the ground had gone, demolished to make way for a new housing estate. Enquiries eventually led me to their new pitch (to now call it a 'ground' would breach the Trade Descriptions Act), squeezed in between modern building developments. This only added to the sense of melancholia which at least took my mind off my still distended gut.

Only slowly was I beginning to adapt to changes, to places having vanished, or been redeveloped. At this stage I still took it as an affront, and against the natural order. I was still clinging on because I could not let go of the past, even though the past had long since let go of me. In Nottingham, not a trace of young Mortimer remained.

Sunday and therefore no *bon mots* today from the *Nottingham Post*.

MONDAY APRIL 25

SOCIAL CLIMBING
AND THE FOOTIE DOG

For the first time in forty-six years I was living in a place where the native accent was my own. I had grown accustomed, first as a student in Sheffield, then as a fledgling journalist in East London, and finally as a journalist-turned-writer on Tyneside, to people asking me "so where are you from originally?" This was due partly to the Nottingham accent being among the lowest profile in the country. Also my own version had become tempered over the years by Yorkshire, Cockney and Geordie.

Now, almost half a century on, and back on home ground, I was wallowing in sounding like everyone else. Each day I felt my accent grow broader, reflecting some deep need to be accepted once more by my native city. Having a different accent to most of those around you, as had been my case for almost half a century, brought a certain sense of the outsider. In the polyglot of London, one of the nation's and indeed the world's great melting pots, this mattered little; the relevance was greater in the more insular culture of Tyneside. I had lived in the small coastal village of Cullercoats for thirty-six years, almost twice as long as my time in Nottingham, yet was still viewed by many Cullercoats locals with the caution reserved for offcomers.

In Nottingham, no-one could doubt my heritage. It was there in every flattened vowel.

Not that I planned to move back to this city, nor had any plans to leave Tyneside.

Yet the city of Nottingham still owned a part of me that no other place could. This had little to do with logic, but my return brought home how much I was proud of my accent, and its ability to survive various geographical shifts.

I knew one well-known Tyneside actor who in the space of a year deliberately modified his 'natural' accent to become RP. This was a career move, the motivation being he was being pigeon-holed for only Geordie parts. There may have been a certain logic to this, but through this verbal metamorphosis he became a strange hybrid, so that when talking to him I was convinced he was playing some kind of role, and any moment would break off with the phrase "Hadaway, man! Nee Geordie taaaks lake that!" and revert to normality. Except he had created a new (and slightly disturbing) normality.

My father deliberately panel-beat his own Nottingham accent out of existence. As his one-man business expanded from the front room of our council house, where he wrapped and despatched nylons direct to the public, as he climbed the social ladder and made inroads into the Nottingham business fraternity (joining the golf club was one tactical move) so his accent changed. The very nature of his vowels altered, he spoke slower, more deliberately. The deep clunking 'u' sound as in 'bus' or 'lump' became lightweight, almost fragrant. The short 'a' sound as in 'dance' stretched itself out to 'darnce'. He also spoke more politely than was the norm on this estate. I was puzzled by this and wondered if there was a natural time in life when you crossed a border into the realms of the well-mannered.

Like my actor friend, my father saw the whole exercise as a means of progression, as if truly we do judge people by the way certain sounds come out of their mouth.

I had now been on Danethorpe Vale for a week. Derrick and Valerie had been open, generous and flexible in adapting to the unusual requirements of a writer invading their home, and they left me undisturbed whenever I locked myself away in my room to scribble. An author by necessity spends much time alone, but outside of the actual writing I was a social animal who yearned for company, and shrivelled up without human interaction.

Peter the clown, with Alex and Minnie Mort, in a theatre production in Cullercoats during the 1980s.

And I felt strangely isolated on the estate. Apart from the washing machine repair man, no visitor had ventured through the door. I had met no neighbours, not even Derrick Junior, whose voice I heard on his daily visit to the doorstep. Why was I unusually abashed in approaching him? Was it the disturbing sight of my erstwhile home, the now dilapidated 97 Danethorpe Vale? Was I afraid of what may lie inside that house?

Nothing prevented me simply knocking on Derrick Junior's or other neighbours' doors and announcing myself. Hadn't I displayed the very same brazen cheek a month long for my book *Broke Through Britain,* when daily I was driven by necessity to knock on the doors of total strangers for food, shelter and warmth?

Yet on Sherwood Estate such behaviour seemed wrong, unnatural. Had I been here as a detached journalist, or a documentary maker out to do a professional job painting the contemporary social, economic and political life on this estate, fine. But it was more personal than that. This had been my home. This place was deep in my veins, yet simultaneously seemed to be telling me that, once outside the safe confines of number 85, I was no part of it. I could not resolve that dilemma simply by knocking on doors clutching a notebook. Such behaviour would confirm me as an outsider, a voyeur, which is possibly what I now was.

On that particular day, I was gripped by a strange panic, as if there may simply be nothing I could do except get in the car and drive away from Sherwood Estate.

Which is exactly what I did, though I was heading back north for only three miles. I needed to connect with something familiar. The pinnacle of my Nottingham football career had been with Arnold St. Mary's FC, then of the semi-professional Midlands League. They were now renamed Arnold Town, and in the Northern Counties East Premier league, no longer at their Gedling Road ground. To make way for a property redevelopment which had still not taken place, they had been despatched more

76

than two miles outside Arnold into the countryside near Calverton.

A fine new ground it was too, in some ways, with training pitches, bar and recreation facilities, yet it was all wrong. A team such as Arnold, from a tight working-class community, required a ground that reflected that community and was based in it, not untimely ripped from its natural soil. The backdrop to the new ground was not terraced housing but fields of rape. And how did the fans get there? There was a big car park, but traditionally most Arnold fans were not car owners and walked to the ground. And no special bus service was laid on for matches. The next evening Arnold were playing Hallam FC from Sheffield and if they lost would be relegated. It suddenly seemed a sorry tale, me and Arnold Town, both misplaced. The least I could do the next day was come back and shout my support.

The Arnold experience led me immediately to seek out another of my former clubs, Gedling Miners' Welfare FC, for whom I'd played just one season in the early sixties, one of six clubs in my peripatetic Nottingham football career. Local football was a grass roots activity close to my heart, and in many ways more a barometer of the nation's well-being than the inflated artificialities of the Premier League. I'd been disturbed by Arnold Town being sacrificed on the altar of commercial developers, and in recent days the *Nottingham Post* announced other sad news. Eastwood Town, one of the most prominent non-league teams hereabouts, was up for sale for £1. Ilkeston Town had folded and Hucknall Town were facing closure due to lack of local volunteers to run the club. This news led me to expect the worst at Gedling, where financial backing had once come from the now vanished coal industry

I was pleasantly surprised to find the football club still in rude health. The modern compact ground was situated on Mapperley Plains, a misnomer as the road was in fact a high spine, falling away spectacularly each side, affording some of the best views Nottingham could offer: in one direction across Woodthorpe and Arnold, and to the east across the beautiful rolling countryside to Gedling and beyond. The club had once been generously supported by the NCB which meant excellent facilities for the players. I was not a miner, but they let me in the team anyway. The coal industry had collapsed, but not so the club, currently second in the Central Midlands Supreme Division (words such as Premier, Supreme and Paramount had long since replaced the simple description 'First') with high ambitions of moving up the soccer pyramid.

In 1951, its heyday, Gedling attracted a crowd of 10,000 in an Amateur Cup game against Bishop Auckland, still a record for a Nottinghamshire amateur club, and in 2011 it was still ambitious, a family (or families) affair involving the Hulmes, the Osbornes and the Hays. My unannounced visit at 1pm afforded me an instant tour from club activist Alan Bush. I reminded Alan I played for Gedling all those years ago.

"Peter Mortimer? Of course. One of the best midfielders we ever had. Boy, we were silly to let you go to Arnold. People still talk about your silky skills." How nice if Alan had spoken those words. As it was, he shook his head and said, "No, the name don't ring no bells." This fitted the pattern of my Nottingham return.

I told Alan I was off to see Notts County play Brentford that afternoon. Disappointment momentarily crossed his face, a disappointment that hinted the man may actually have cared that I was not planning to stay for the Gedling game. This look of disappointment stayed with me as I cycled the two miles back down to the estate and Danethorpe Vale, parked the bike, walked the half mile up Edwards Lane to Mansfield Road, bought myself a ham cob, ate the cob and stood waiting outside the Co-op for the bus. In the next two minutes that look of disappointment became all-pervasive. I walked back the half mile down Edwards Lane to Danethorpe Vale, picked up

78

the bike, cycled the mountainously steep two miles back up Breckhill Road to Mapperley Plains, locked up the bike and paid my entrance fee to see Gedling Miners' Welfare play their local derby against Gedling Town. Alan Bush was taking the money

"Yo decided to come back then?" he said.

"'Ar," I said.

Three things stand out from that 2–0 victory, attended by a crowd of just over 100, and observed by me from my seat in the small new stand. Firstly in the tea bar, Janine Osborne, who ran the bar with her daughter Chaleigh, agreed to sell me the official club clock for a fiver, which now graces my kitchen back in Cullercoats. Secondly, Gedling Town's trainer was female, blonde, wearing tight denim shorts and a shoulderless boob-tube top. When she ran on to treat a player the wag nearby commented, "them boggers'll all be getting injured nah!"

Thirdly, for the first time in my life I watched a football match with a dog in the seat next to me, a black Labrador who barked in displeasure at every offside decision.

On the other side sat the club kitman, eighty-five-year-old Harold Hulme, who had been with the club since the mid-

Janine Osborne, the bringer of time

1950s, or to put it another way, for almost a decade before anyone had heard of The Beatles. Harold didn't remember the silky skills of Peter Mortimer either. Janine Osborne told me her friend Sandra lived on Dane-thorpe Vale, and I should call round. I did, later on, but after a few minutes talking on the doorstep to her and her

79

husband, I made my slightly awkward farewells and left. What had I expected? To be invited in, offered a drink, made a fuss of? Probably. I still didn't get in.

The mood, as the previous night, darkened as I drank in the all-but-deserted Five Ways, my only short conversation being with the barman John when he told me there was no slice of lime to go with my bottle of Corona beer. Corona, incidentally, was also the name of an erstwhile Nottingham soft drinks manufacturer. I finished the drink and left, the only slightly cheery moment being when I held the loo door open for an elderly gent. "Alright then?" I asked.

"'Ar, lad," he replied. 'Lad' — I quite liked that.

Derrick and Valerie were already in bed when I got home. By the way, Notts County had played out a dull 0–0 draw with Brentford that afternoon. No sexy trainer. No disapproving dog.

THIS NOTTINGHAM

A Nottingham woman has broken the world record for being a surrogate mother to a monkey. Andrea Donaldson has so far kept the monkey alive for 81 days (previous best 55 days) by wrapping it in a sarong and feeding it goat's milk and wild flowers.

TUESDAY APRIL 26

THE BARD AND THE LINIMENT

It was sheet changing and washing day at number 85 Danethorpe Vale. Valerie was in full flow upstairs, and preparing to strip and change my bed when I stepped in and stopped her. Did she not realise she was in the company of a fully domesticated male, able to carry out such tasks for himself?

I am a compulsive bed-maker, unable to walk from the room till the bed is neatly remade, corners tucked in tight. The thought of passing the day with the bed unmade is abhorrent, an obsession causing much merriment with my partner Kitty, who could happily leave an unmade bed hours long the shape of a tossed sea, and even when she made it, decline to tuck in the corners, seeing this as unnecessary confinement.

I also took a quiet delight in contemplating the newly made bed, standing back to view it, as if a small part of the universe had been given a sense of smoothed order. Any tiny crease spotted would be gently flattened out, giving the universe a proper sense of purpose. Thus I replaced the sheets myself this day, though some kind of compromise was reached, with Valerie bunging the old ones in the washing machine.

For the first time that morning I exchanged a few words with the by-now-mythical son, Derrick Junior. He was at the door, exchanging the daily slightly acrimonious words with his father when I introduced myself. Derrick Junior was thin, a shaved head, the slightly nervous energy of a caged animal.

Valerie had suggested he might be ashamed to let me see the interior of number 97, and when I suggested a visit he shrugged his shoulders and said the place was "a bit of a tip." This reaction seemed not totally dismissive

81

of the entire idea, which I then pursued, saying I'd lived in a few tips in my time, so it was no big deal.

"Yo writin' a book?" he asked and I said yes, I was. That was more or less the end of our initial exchange which, I told myself, was not entirely disastrous.

I was tugged this day towards experiencing something cultural. I decided to call at Nottingham Playhouse and the Theatre Royal and Concert Hall.

There had been a Playhouse in Nottingham since the 1940s, but the new building was opened in 1963 with a production of Shakespeare's *Coriolanus,* a brave choice, directed by the legendary Tyrone Guthrie. The artistic directors at that time were John Neville, Peter Ustinov and Frank Dunlop, an impressive trio to be running a provincial theatre. The birth of the new Nottingham Playhouse was an important landmark in the development of postwar British drama, a fact of which I had been blissfully ignorant at the time, devoting much more attention to slurping down Shippo's bitter.

I could still remember the previous Nottingham Playhouse in Goldsmith Street, where as thirteen year olds, we school children had been herded in and force-fed live performances of Shakespeare, a policy breeding huge resentment against our greatest ever writer, and the conclusion that he was obscure and boring. Witness my extremely short poem, 'Stratford Visit' — *Bard/Stiff.*

It took years of cultural transformation for me to appreciate the poetic and dramatic power of the man. I was lucky enough to become a drama critic for a period, which helped, but as a nation we are still uneasy about Shakespeare. With many audiences, as the plays open, there's a slight unease that they may simply not 'get it'. Much of this is born from their confused childhood exposure. My solution? Ban Shakespeare early on. Later, make him compulsory.

The old Playhouse was now a bar with the wondrous name Spanky Van Dykes ('Eatery and Funhouse') and its successor was in Canning Street.

When my brother started reading *The Guardian,* while the rest of us were still digesting pap from the red tops, he pointed out that the newspaper included theatre reviews from the Nottingham Playhouse. I was mightily impressed that such a cultured and lofty organ should even visit humble Nottingham. Had anyone then told me I would later become the North-East theatre critic for *The Guardian*, I'd have chinned them for being a leary git.

Nor did I have any idea that theatre would become such an essential part of my own life. Nor that I would become a full-time writer. Such things did not happen to boys from Sherwood Estate, and to the end of their lives both my mother and father wondered why I had given up proper work to pursue scribbling.

But there was an early clue. I still have on my bookshelf a copy of the book *Captain of Hungary* by Ferenc Puskás. On the inside front page is pasted a High Pavement School Prize label dated Dec 5, 1955 stating the book was awarded to Mortimer P. (Sherwood House) for storytelling. It is signed by the headteacher, H. Davies. More glittering literary prizes, let me add, failed to materialise.

My journey from Nottingham to the worlds beyond was a gradual appreciation of that most derided of words — culture. Where initially culture was, at best, of marginal influence on my life and, at worst, irrelevant, later it was to become an essential, something one admits to in the culturally cynical UK with a certain apprehension. And this day, as in affirmation of the same, I did what I had never done while living twenty-one years in this city; I booked tickets for shows at the Playhouse, the Theatre Royal, and the Royal Concert Hall. To be fair, the last did not even exist then.

After which I made my way to Clarendon Street, in the north-east central part of the city, close to the beautiful Arboretum, and an area now almost swallowed whole by Nottingham Trent University. At the bottom of Clarendon Street — number 60 — were the premises of my first post-school employer, Arthur E. Inger Ltd, Suppliers to the Dental Trade. The school careers notice board had advertised for someone with modern language to A-level standard for a sales career in the city, the country and eventually the world, a job description which was to prove in almost every word as false as the million teeth the firm claimed to have in stock.

In eighteen months employed by Arthur E. Inger Ltd, Suppliers to the Dental Trade, under the title of 'trainee salesman', my language skills were called in to translate two letters into English, nothing more. I sold nothing to anybody, and lived a semi-troglodyte existence in the despatch room basement, a time which only later proved to have any purpose when I used the setting for an early play, *The Man Who Played With Mice*. This premièred in a tiny theatre in Austin, Texas, and played also in a marginally bigger theatre in Tynemouth, after which its anticipated seismic effect on contemporary British drama failed to materialise.

By some process of which I was ignorant, this basement 'training' was supposed to gradually equip me for a life on the road as a salesman. Ingers was a small firm with branches in Leicester and Sheffield, run by the eponymous owner, a small, dapper Jewish man with gold-rimmed spectacles who lived in a big house in Redhill.

My father, determined I should succeed in the commercial field which was obviously the natural hunting ground of elder brother Alex, leant on the firm to allow me day release for the same business qualification for which Alex was studying. With his A-levels in Latin and Ancient Greek, Alex was the bright light of the estate, a young man forging a promising career at Meridian Ltd, one of the city's leading hosiery manufacturers. Meridian sent Alex on the HNC (Business Studies) course at the Nottingham Technical College (now the hub of Nottingham Trent University). This took three years to complete, comprising three nights and a full day's study every week. For some reason Arthur E. Inger Ltd allowed me on it too.

On the course I was surrounded by young high-fliers from Raleigh, Boots, Players, Ericksons, leading Nottingham companies investing in their managerial talent of the future. When I announced my own employer, the universal reaction was "who?" When I told them the firm sold false teeth, and their letterhead bore the slogan 'More than a million teeth in stock!' they tended to sidle away.

Those in later life who took me as some kind of arty-farty dilettante writer with no grasp of the real world, were often surprised to know of this Business Studies qualification, not to mention an honours degree in Economics gained later at Sheffield University, proof if any were needed that education is often best found in areas unrelated to your work.

Fifty years on, 60 Clarendon Street looked pretty much the same. A four storey red-brick terrace of somewhat imposing ecclesiastical appearance with its vaulted main door and windows and grand set of ten steps up to the main entrance, it was now part of the university, closed for the holidays, and with a highly complex entry security code. A faint hope that the rear entrance might allow me a glimpse of the fabled basement was soon dashed. And the nearby Post Office to which I daily carried parcels of vital dental supplies, was no more.

Mr Inger had eventually called me into his office and sacked me. The intellectual demands of wrapping up false teeth proved so meagre that the quality of my work deteriorated. Nor did the prospect of me going out on the road as a salesman seem any nearer. I was at a dead end. Laughable though it may now seem, when I started work for Inger's with a ten shilling (50p) yearly rise on my £6 per week starting salary I calculated what my wage would be on retirement. Thus my soaring ambition.

When I announced news of the sacking to my father, he retorted, "There are nearly three hundred thousand people unemployed in this country, and you get yourself sacked! So what will you do now?" I had no idea, but the same night in The Five Ways I won a few bob at darts, which was some small compensation.

Oh, and I did carry on with and pass the HNC.

Another, slightly better known, writer had mixed fortunes in this area. Graham Greene lived for four months in Nottingham in 1925/26 close to the Arboretum while working as an unpaid trainee sub-editor of the *Nottingham Journal*. Greene was writing a novel which was never published, though he did set an early published novel in the city, *This Gun for Hire*. There is a tendency for novelists, when setting their work in Nottingham, to give the city a false name, a tradition Greene upheld by calling it Nottwich.

First published in 1936, and termed 'An Entertainment' this is a fairly cold-blooded thriller about the murderer Raven, who assassinates a foreign Minister of War, enabling certain parties to make a killing in the armaments business. When his rich and powerful hirers double-cross him, Raven goes hunting for them — a hunt which leads to Nottwich, described with not a shred of affection or enthusiasm by the author. Brief references to the Castle, Robin Hood, the Market Square and the daily newspapers establish Nottingham as the only possibility for the location, but it's a dark, grimy, unloving city Greene portrays.

Always readable, the book's not Greene at his best, though the embittered Raven (who is burdened with a hare lip) seems the prototype for Pinkie, the anti-hero of Greene's next novel *Brighton Rock*. And it's a long time since I read the description of tough guys as 'he-men.'

Greene's feelings for Nottingham were expressed colourfully in Norman Sherry's official biography where his (Greene's) comments include 'an educated person in Nottingham is as precious and rare to find as jam in a wartime doughnut,' and he refers to the city as 'a place undisturbed by ambition, a place to be resigned to.' Despite such disparaging remarks, there is a plaque to the author on the newspaper's one-time premises in

Upper Parliament Street — though the plaque is not of the blue variety.

I drove again to Eagle Valley, the new home of Arnold Town FC, the only club of my erstwhile Nottingham football sextet where I got paid, albeit the 'boot' money was hardly life-changing. For me Arnold represented the giddy heights, and during one training session a player was pointed out who had been signed for a four-figure fee from Lincoln City. Never had I been close to such an elevated personage. He took on heroic proportions even though, as a humble member of the reserve team, I never got to speak to him.

Arnold Town were playing the Sheffield team Norton FC, and if they failed to get a point would be relegated from their league's premier division. If Norton failed to win they would suffer the same fate, so something had to give in a needle match attracting the season's largest crowd of 159. They'd only printed sixty programmes, all long gone by the time of my arrival.

This wind-swept new rural location offered few traditional reminders for a man seeking some grasp of the past. Only the incredible heaviness of the turnstiles, needing Herculean strength to push, reminded me of days gone by, plus the entry sign with the words 'Old Age Pensioners £2.'

'One senior citizen," I said, defiantly pushing forward my loot.

It was a bad-tempered game, foul language streaming from the mouths of both sides, a modern trait which the game seems unable or willing to combat. I don't wish to be a Grumpy Old Man, but I recalled the Corinthian traditions of the Midland Amateur Alliance, where I played for Sherwood Amateurs. Any four-letter word would have brought dismissal, and at the final whistle, each skipper would shout, "Three cheers for the Old Bridgfordians!" or whatever the opposition.

At the interval, Arnold were winning 2–1, the temperature had dropped ten degrees, the wind was whipping in from the rape fields, and in the bar I sought out the club president Alan Croome, while I slurped down the hot powdery tomato soup (80p) in an attempt to unfreeze the bones. How did Alan feel about his club being forced to move more than two miles out into the countryside to make way for a supermarket development which two years on had not happened?

"How would you feel? The club's not what it was. How are our supporters supposed to get here? Something like this knocks the stuffing out of you."

A small clutch of Norton supporters had made the seventy-mile round trip. One quartet included two men in straw boaters, a third wearing a shiny red devil's mask, and a fourth dressed as what I took to be a giant pink blancmange. They were armed with those inflatable fairground hammers with which they regularly beat each other about the head, simultaneously guffawing. This touch of childlike innocence slightly diluted the aggressive blaspheming elsewhere.

Arnold eventually won 2–1, and relegation was staved off. But what, I wondered, did the future hold for this windy outpost?

No-one at this club remembered me. Arnold FC now played no part in my life. Yet I felt strangely concerned as to its fate. I could still smell the pungent liniment of the dressing room, could still hear the clomp-clomp of boots across the wooden floors, still feel the certain frisson as I pulled on the club shirt.

For each and every game during my football career I created in my head two pieces of journalism, a preliminary one looking forward to the tussle ahead, and afterwards a match report, complete with headline, giving a step-by-step description of the ninety minutes of action. Naturally these reports were liberally sprinkled with mentions of the silky skills of a certain inside forward, Peter Mortimer. At the time I was convinced all this was a preparation for me becoming a professional footballer. Now I see it was a preparation for me becoming a professional writer.

THIS NOTTINGHAM

University of Nottingham Biochemics Laboratory has conducted Easter experiments on Cadbury Creme Eggs, putting them through compression and impact tests.

WEDNESDAY APRIL 27

HIDDEN LITERARY TALENTS AS MORTIMER GETS CHEESY

Outside my window, the cherry tree was blowing its dreamy clouds of pink blossom across Danethorpe Vale, adding to the ghostly sense of unreality which that view created in me. Each morning Valerie prepared breakfast for herself and us two men of the house. Normally it was porridge sprinkled with pumpkin seeds followed by toast and tea, and served prompt at 9am.

Normally I would rise early — by about 7am — enabling me to get in both a pre-breakfast writing and a yoga session.

While preparing breakfast this morning Valerie said, "Actually, I've written a book." The tone was casual, yet writing a book was never a casual pursuit. She wrote the book during her teacher-training years, and it was called *The Tree*.

Each page was hand-written and Valerie's own illustrations were mounted alongside. The book had a card cover and had also been bound by hand, overall a creation of some loving care and attention. The story spanned five hundred years, the life of one oak tree, beginning with the single seed of an acorn, and ending with the tree being cut down and made into public benches. During those five hundred years the book followed successive generations of one family as seen through the different fortunes of the tree; the people would flirt by it, snooze under it, hold meetings by it, some were even hanged from it.

I liked the story and the structure and suggested ways it could be developed. This was commonplace behaviour for me as an editor, but clearly not for Valerie who first looked embarrassed, and then feigned indifference, laughing it off with, "Oh, well, I don't know — it's nothing really..."

It *was* something of course, but as I knew from my past, culture and the estate weren't always easy bedfellows. I suspected few people were aware of the book. Later when Derrick saw it in the living room he asked what it was. I told him it was Valerie's book, but he knew nothing about it. I brought the subject up with Valerie a couple more times, but steadily the book returned to the anonymity whence it had arrived.

On this evening I'd promised to cook the tea myself, giving Valerie a break from the stonking great meals she dished up daily. These traditional offerings of sausage, egg and chips, lamb or pork chops and three veg were always substantial portions, but also followed by the likes of sherry trifle and custard, combinations capable of anchoring you to your chair.

"Don't cook anything too fancy," Valerie said. And I decided on the unique Mortimer cheese and potato pie, a culinary delight whose recipe I have now passed on to my son Dylan. I can heartily recommend it; for three people you require two pounds of potatoes, a pound of mature cheddar, one beaten egg, two onions chopped fine, butter, milk, English mustard, a sprinkle of marjoram, a large tomato sliced thinly, and one tin of tomatoes. Mash the spuds, grate in most of the cheese, add onions, lightly fried, marjoram, beaten egg, butter and milk, heat in a hot oven for fifteen minutes, sprinkle the rest of the cheese on top along with the tomato slices, heat under grill for five minutes, serve with heated tinned tomatoes. Lovely!

Both Valerie and Derrick asked for seconds, which pleased me immensely. In the tradition of the house I followed this main course with a treacle pudding and custard, which was also effectively despatched.

I'd bought the food at the Hucknall Road Co-op where between the ages of 13-16 I'd earned a meagre pittance as a grocery delivery boy, riding one of those heavy black bikes with a front carrier. This experience obviously stayed with me. I bought a similar model in Cullercoats and would carry young Dylan in the front wicker basket till he grew too large to fit, and the bike began to fall to bits.

That afternoon my publisher Ross Bradshaw called. We sat in the still deserted Valley Road Park, and I mentioned how busy it had been in my childhood.

"Valley Road itself is a natural barrier now," said Ross. He was right. Crossing the Le Mans track of Valley Road, even with the pedestrian lights, was not a feat to be engaged in lightly. Sherwood Estate was surrounded by roads of fierce and constant traffic, Valley Road, Mansfield Road, Hucknall Road, the vehicles swirling past like fast-flowing water round an isolated rock.

That evening, Derrick, Valerie and I watched the European Cup semi-final between Real Madrid and Barcelona. It was as bad-tempered as Arnold Town v Norton FC, though with around 100,000 spectators in the Bernabeu as against 159 at Eagle Valley, it was hard to hear if the players were constantly blaspheming. Plus which my Spanish wasn't that hot.

THIS NOTTINGHAM

At an event at Greens Windmill, Sneinton, children can pretend to be bugs.

THURSDAY APRIL 28

THE OAK IS DEAD, LONG LIVE THE OAK

Royal Wedding fever was growing for the next day, as the UK prepared to show the world how brilliant it was at staging its Ruritanian ceremonies.

Even this morning more than 1,900 of the country's richest and most influential people would be laying out their togs in preparation for the beanfeast. If we were truly a democracy then fifty per cent of the tickets could have been put up as National Lottery prizes. If this meant Elton John *et al.* had to miss this particular jolly so be it. There would be plenty more for them, and why *not* have a few unemployed welders from Scunthorpe in the Westminster Abbey audience?

Maybe it was Valerie's tree story that decided me to drive out to Edwinstowe to see The Major Oak, Nottingham's one living link with its own royalty, Robin Hood. I say 'living' though the word may be a mite optimistic given the poor tree's geriatric state. Euthanasia may have been the more merciful solution, but the oak's symbolism for the city was such that this was not an option. The Major Oak featured on the Notts County Council logo, as the logo of Nottingham Building Society, on beer bottle labels, and many other places. The Robin Hood industry was thriving; the *Nottingham Post* had the subhead 'City of Legends' plus a small silhouette of the famous archer, and until recent times Nottingham Forest ran out to the cheesy sounds of the song *Robin Hood* from the 1960s' TV series. The city was liberally sprinkled with streets, pubs and cafés bearing the names of Robin Hood, Little John, Maid Marian, Will Scarlet, and Friar Tuck.

The Royal Oak itself was reputed to be up to 1,000 years old. If true this would mean it first sprouted while

Ethelred I was on the throne.

When living in Sherwood, you would occasionally be hailed by passing tourists seeking out the forest. I would enjoy their looks of disappointment when I directed them twenty miles north. Sherwood Forest had once been one of Europe's biggest natural forests at 100,000 acres, but now at 450 acres, was one-fiftieth its original size. And was nowhere near Sherwood.

Visiting the Major Oak was a peaceful and pleasurable experience; park up in the village of Edwinstowe, then a one-mile walk through woodland paths, a tranquil odyssey to pay homage to the old fellow (the oak definitely seemed male).

This walk had a strange spectral quality. On both sides of the trail, I passed the distinctive and haunting-looking stag-head oaks, ancient trees that had been eaten alive from the inside by termites, leaving their sharply angled shapes dramatically silhouetted against the sky like giant insects. They had been petrified, turned to stone.

Stag-head oaks

Reduced in size the forest may be, but it still offers the country's best concentration of ancient oaks. In 1666 Sir Christopher Wren rebuilt St Paul's cathedral using Sherwood Oak, and — a fact not many people know — this forest could boast of more than 200 species of spider.

The Major Oak itself was estimated to weigh 23 tons, and was not particularly tall, more the squat posture of a sumo wrestler, the huge trunk resembling crumpled folds of old elephant skin. The tree was now supported on crutches of a discreet eco-green colour, giving the impression of some terribly old gentleman precariously staying on his feet.

As lads we would travel here and huddle inside the hollow centre where Robin is said to have hidden from the Sheriff of Nottingham and met up with his merry men (why the adjective 'merry'? I never understood). We once crammed thirteen bodies inside. This was no longer possible. In 1969 the ground surrounding the oak, trampled to sterility by millions of feet, was fenced off, and the soil had now returned to fertility. But how alive was the tree itself? It had just come into leaf, but the leaves were sickly and weak-looking, as if some huge effort were required for them to sprout.

Close by was the inevitable tourist centre with shops and cafés, though the forest itself remained blissfully peaceful and uncrowded, the only idiosyncrasy being the small fairground, its stalls, rides and fast food vans

The Major Oak

95

sitting incongruously among the greenery. There were few takers, including myself, which, ridiculously, made me feel guilty. As I walked past each stallholder, their plaintive 'please stay!' looks pursued me, I resisted the urge continually to say, "Sorry!"

Driving north out of Nottingham, the last built-up area on Mansfield Road is Redhill, where my parents moved post-Sherwood-Estate. They initially bought a house called Cherry Holt, and later sold it, keeping part of the spacious garden in which to build a new bungalow. These were to be their last two residences before their final dismal years in care homes, to pay for which their new house had to be sold. There was a certain irony to this, all those years striving to break into the property-owning classes, and for what?

I was constantly wracked with guilt that my brother Alex and I had dumped our parents, yet without knowing what alternative we could have chosen. The painful practicalities of dealing with parental decline fell mainly to Alex and his wife Helen, who eventually moved them to a Rotherham care home half a mile from their own residence. Being 135 miles distant on Tyneside, my part was the occasional overnight visit.

That evening I cycled the three miles to the two houses, both in Monsell Drive, Redhill. During the ride an incredible weariness came over me, legs heavy and aching, energy levels reduced. I reached Monsell Drive to find the owners of the second property away on holiday. What had been an open driveway to the house now had high locked gates.

The householder in Cherry Holt answered the door and I realised we had met before. For a few moments we chatted on the doorstep, I spoke of my memories of this house (where I lived for two years), but there was no move to invite me in.

On my return cycle journey, the weariness grew, as did the sense that Nottingham was not accepting my return. I had now knocked at three separate doors without once being invited in. And I had still been unable to cross the threshold of number 97, the house I grew up in. Derrick Junior did not cross the threshold of number 85, where his father lived, nor did his father or Valerie venture into number 97. What chance for me?

I thought back to Shatila Palestinian Refugee Camp in Beirut, a squalid place where one of the few things in generous supply was hospitality. To call at any household, and not to be invited in, not to be offered refreshment, and to stay for less than an hour was unheard of. Of course, most people in Shatila dreamed of living in our affluent West.

Was I simply experiencing the colder, more reticent English? Did this behaviour suggest I should never have returned? I had received hospitality and kindness from Valerie and Derrick, but elsewhere, ten days in, had failed to break the skin of Sherwood Estate.

My return journey from Redhill took me past the cemetery where my mother and father were buried. I had visited their graveside three times, on each occasion with a sense of disquiet little understood. It was on this third visit I realised I hated commemorating my parents this way. To stand in front of this cold piece of stone in this vast field of the dead brought not a flicker of warmth, nor any association to their lives. There was only a sense of morbidity, of silence, of decaying flesh beneath my feet. I was indulging a ritual, a Christian expectation, yet for me the experience was spiritually deadening. This graveyard had nothing to do with their lives, only their deaths. Thoughts, smells, sounds, places, people; these were how I kept their memory. I hurried away from that forbidding place knowing I would never indulge this cold ritual again. I was sad, but had uncovered an important personal truth.

Another ritual was visiting The Five Ways. So important had this pub been in my Sherwood Estate upbringing, so familiar still was its present physicality that I clung to it unnaturally. And in The Five Ways, the

97

saga of the lime slices was about to unfold. I had taken to drinking bottles of Sol or Corona beers, traditionally served with a slice of lime wedged in the top. On the last two occasions no lime was to be had. I enquired mildly as to this ongoing unavailability.

"Limes cost fotty pence each," said barman John, "Not gunna gerrum if the gunna be wasted." I drank the Sol lime-free and decided that in future I would bring my own supplies. The next day I bought five limes for a quid, and kept them in my bag.

The Five Ways had declared Friday a Royal Wedding Free Zone. This seemed a novel concept, and I asked if there were plans for alternative distractions, with a wild thought I could add to them with some comic performance poetry, and hence firm up my relationship with the pub.

"Wu doin' noat," said John, and walked away. There was a finality to this statement that made the pursuit of my own idea seem ridiculous, and brought the growing suspicion I was living in cloud cuckoo land.

THIS NOTTINGHAM

William and Kate Brown from Southwell, Notts are one of 20 couples sharing the same first names as the Royal couple being offered a free week-end away by Travelodge.

FRIDAY APRIL 29

THE ROYALS, THE HEAVENS ABOVE, AND KAFKA

Royal Wedding day, and I awoke with the energy of a discarded dishcloth. For once the urge to leap from bed and begin writing was absent. Limbs ached and I had the overwhelming desire to do nothing, or preferably less. Valerie and Derrick were about early. Derrick was a keen Royalist, Valerie only slightly less. Our relationship by now was relaxed enough to joke about such differences.

At 9am I rose for breakfast, moving downstairs like an exhausted slug. I watched twenty minutes of the wall-to-wall wedding coverage before slinking back to bed. Despite my non-Royalist tendencies, there was something slightly infectious about the uncomplicated celebration and enthusiasm of those who had camped days long on the Mall and elsewhere, an uninhibited delight, against which my own republican grumps could make me sound like a joyless curmudgeon.

I was feeling isolated and insecure on my Nottingham return, and here were other people enjoying a true camaraderie and sense of community camped out on a hard pavement. Ours was a troubled country, often bad-tempered, divided. We could seem to be on a short, potentially destructive fuse. Compare this to the pure uncynical delight of those people on the TV screen, albeit such delight was towards an unelected, privileged, and historically anachronistic dynasty.

Much of the day was spent in bed, spells of fitful sleep interrupted by Derrick's occasional excited downstairs shout as the Royal splendour unfolded on the telly, "Cum 'n' look at this, Valerie!"

Late afternoon I stirred myself, and after an unsuccessful attempt at writing — the words falling lumpenly onto the page — walked the two miles for tea at the home of my publisher, Ross Bradshaw. Ross and his partner Myra live to the east above Sherwood close to Mapperley Top, and the quickest pedestrian route was up through Private Road, an aptly named thoroughfare full of impressively large detached houses. A barrier at the top, opened only with a residents' pass, kept out the motoring hoi-polloi, though pedestrians could enjoy freedom of passage denied to non-residential car drivers.

My memories of Private Road involved Christmas, and the Hucknall Road Co-op delivery boy job (why were there never delivery girls?). Demand for turkeys saw us lads whizzing the big birds all over Sherwood on our black bikes. We were given Christmas boxes in plenty on Sherwood Estate and surrounds, though the most meagre pickings came from the big houses on Private Road, so each of us would attempt to offload these deliveries onto the others.

Private Road, and its sense of hushed opulence, had altered hardly at all, but then it had little reason to. Wealth brought less desire for, or need of change (it wasn't called The Conservative Party for nothing), and places such as Private Road were rarely troubled with the likes of Compulsory Purchase Orders, or redevelopment dictats. You'd just as soon see them building on the local private golf clubs. Local football clubs however (like Arnold Town FC) were a different matter.

After tea and sympathy with Ross and Myra, I made my way to Nottingham Playhouse, close to which was St Barnabas, probably one of the country's least known or recognised cathedrals. I had recently visited one of my favourite UK buildings, Liverpool's Metropolitan Cathedral, a fantastical space ship soaring up from the top of Hope Street, a visionary edifice, a flying saucer, or Paddy's wigwam as the locals affectionately nicknamed it. Against this breathless vision, St. Barnabas seemed a crouched recluse, turning its face from the world. Though brought up a Catholic in Nottingham, not once had I

100

set foot in it. Graham Greene did, being converted to Catholicism there.

Close by, outside The Playhouse itself, was the modern sculpture, *The Sky Mirror*, Amish Kapoor's huge tilted silver dish. This reflected and opened up for the viewer the firmaments, seeming to remove him or her from an earthbound existence in the way a cathedral should, and which Liverpool could, but of which the very grounded St Barnabas looked singularly incapable.

I had a ticket for Stephen Berkoff's version of Franz Kafka's *The Trial*, performed by the Nottingham Playhouse Youth Theatre.

After I first left Nottingham I began reading in earnest, and Kafka was among the writers who opened doors for me. *The Trial* is the claustrophobic tale of Joseph K, arrested early one morning, yet never able to discover his supposed crime, as the judicial system slowly closes in on him, eventually with dire consequences. It has the memorable opening words, 'Someone must have been spreading lies about Joseph K.'

The adjective 'Kafkaesque' is chucked around too freely, though this was not the fault of the books. In Kafka's work, people inhabit worlds utterly ordinary, yet simultaneously terrifying, especially in *The Trial* and *Metamorphosis,* both of which haunted me, and later influenced my own novella *Uninvited*. Here was a perspective on urban life I had never experienced, a dimension of which I was ignorant, people crying out with voices I had never heard yet somehow recognised.

Directed by Sarah Stephenson, the Youth Theatre production was an astonishing mix of high energy discipline and flair. Kafka was given the physical theatre treatment. And over two and a half hours, the twenty youngsters, aged between fourteen and twenty-one, never missed a beat. It was a truly ensemble production, the cast called upon to create sudden friezes or tableaux, to become a row of clattering typewriters, a moving community bus, or a series of paintings in a gallery. Happily,

101

even on that day of mega-nuptials, the auditorium was four-fifths full. Good stuff!

I caught the bus home, where the telly was showing *Fifty Best Wedding Anthems on Video*, which was something different entirely.

THIS NOTTINGHAM

A Hucknall man who wrote to Royal Mail asking where its postboxes were positioned was shocked to be told the that information "could not be released into the public domain." Mr David Heathcote described the decision as "very, very silly."

SATURDAY APRIL 30

THE LONE RANGER
AND THE LONE DANCER

Two things were upsetting Valerie today. The *Nottingham Post*'s lead story was about a fifty-one-year-old Arnold roofer who fell to his death, fuelling her understandable fears about Derrick's occasional work days, scampering about on rooftops wearing no safety gear. The relief she always felt on his return from such work, today was magnified.

Secondly, the new Bosch washing machine installed after the repair man inflicted on the kitchen a flood of biblical proportion, used electricity not gas to heat the water, bypassing her solar energy system, and hence ratcheting up the fuel bills. Not that Valerie was among the world's complainers. She dealt splendidly with my own small quirks, the kind of irritating habits that could lead to domestic murders. Thus, her casual question, "What colour is your electric toothbrush exactly?" when I'd been using hers by mistake, or a gentle reminder I was putting waste in the wrong bin, or splashing water round the base of the electric kettle, or using Derrick's favourite mug. All these potential friction points were gently rerouted and sorted.

I had never spent a month in such close proximity with a previously unknown couple; nor had Valerie and Derrick needed to adapt their own domestic routine for an interloper for the same period. Consequences could have been disastrous. But they weren't.

Why did I feel older in Nottingham than on Tyneside? It took me a while to work it out. On Tyneside I was a working writer, theatre director and publisher. The thought of retirement never entered my head. Nor would it till I dropped dead (at which point I might give it some

103

small consideration). Many of the similar-aged people I mixed with felt the same. Their creative work defined them, and energised them. To think of an artificial cut-off point where they took home the engraved clock and planned for the Saga cruises was laughable. But in Nottingham I was often seen basically as a sixty-seven year-old man. Most people who had reached my age had settled for retirement and all which that implied. Old. Old. Old. Unbearable.

The milkman came to the front door. He was of a similar age to me, so I asked him if he had any early memories of the estate. I had no idea why I asked, as I usually give a wide berth to such anecdotal nostalgia.

"Ah wuz brought up in Sneinton," he said. (Sneinton is in the east of the city). "Guess 'oo ah met in Sneinton one tahm?"

I told him I had no idea.

"The Lone Ranger!" he replied. "'E cum to the Adelphi Cinema!"

Valerie ordered three pints.

While we were talking, Derrick Junior came to the door, and I managed to collar him for a short while. His reluctance to let me cross his threshold seemed not to be weakening. His entire body language resisted the idea. He backed awkwardly down the path as we spoke, a sheepish look on his face, a desire to be not part of this conversation. For the first time I considered the possibility that I might not enter the house of my childhood. I had taken it as read that my persuasive powers would hold sway, not considering how deep and dark might be the waters into which I was wading, or rather, as it was turning out, not wading.

Later that day on the phone, my son Dylan said, "Anyway, you might find it too painful if he did let you in."

The football season was reaching its climax. Nottingham Forest were playing Scunthorpe United, the former with a chance of the play-offs, the latter already relegated. Few towns were less fashionable than Scunthorpe, and their kit was unfashionable too, yellow and black hooped shirts (horizontal stripes belonged to rugby), on the back of which were big white numbered patches. They ran onto the pitch with the fatalism of a condemned man walking to the scaffold, and were hammered 5–1.

Football matches gave me the excuse, in an otherwise fairly healthy diet, to indulge in fast food excesses. I bought a burger dripping with fried onions, squeezing on vast quantities of both mustard and tomato sauce that left my mouth smeared with a lurid orange goo.

It was while gobbling down this high-calorie, low-protein offering that I noticed the bike racks. Football clubs were not known for their social vision, so how encouraging that Nottingham Forest had taken on the environmental concerns of the day, and in an eco-friendly gesture, provided bike racks for their supporters Their expectations though were minimal. In a crowd of 30,000 people there was enough room to secure ten bikes. Number of bikes present? Four.

There was an innate belief in Nottingham that Forest's natural position was in the Premier League. This same expectation had been with Notts County in my young days. Even when in Division Three (North), County could command crowds of 40,000 and attract players of the calibre of England centre forward Tommy Lawton. But the pendulum had swung Forest's way. They were still the only UK club ever to have won the European Cup (now Championship Cup) twice in succession. My allegiance to Notts County would be lifelong, yet to be at Forest's City Ground on a day such as this, with a charged atmosphere, large expectant crowd, the opposition put to the sword, was to acknowledge their status as a 'big' club.

For Notts County today's result brought a familiar situation. Defeated 2–1 at MK Dons, their fate now hung in the balance, dependent on their final home game against

105

the division champions, Brighton FC. I would be there.

That night I went walk-about on Mansfield Road, Sherwood, visiting two hostelries that had been the occasional if not regular watering holes of the young Mortimer, The Sherwood Inn, and the Robin Hood.

Externally neither showed much sign of change, that solid reassuring architecture of the standard English pub, both still with a strong working class feel. Like many pubs the Robin Hood was originally three rooms, and like many had been knocked into one large area. This unnatural creation still seemed to cry out for its original separate spaces. In one part a five-piece outfit, *The Little Giants*, were singing. In another, men watched football on a giant plasma screen, while in a third people were playing the bandits. All these were separate activities, yet had been pushed into one room, like someone putting starters, main course and pudding on the same plate, destroying the individual flavour of all three.

Those watching the band were mainly middle-aged and of stout proportion. Unlike the audience at a paid rock concert, they witnessed each number without a single rhythmic response from their bodies, as if the connection between the music and their nervous system had been severed.

After several numbers a solitary man got up to dance. He was of different appearance, slimmer, lank longish hair, a middle-aged exile from the Summer Festivals, and he danced as if surges of electricity were sent through him. He was impervious to the prominence his solitary dancing attracted. He was possibly fortified in this lack of self-consciousness by various artificial substances. His boldness had an effect. A woman got up and danced with him. She too was younger than most here, her dress sense less 'solid'.

The sight of the two dancing, plus no doubt the alcohol now beginning to kick in, slowly prompted various others who stood up to dance, though dance was perhaps too optimistic a word for the slightly awkward and minimal arm, leg and body movement which seemed less a release,

106

more a piece of mechanics. Minimal though this animation was, it slightly energised the room, or at least that part of it.

The next-door Sherwood Inn was, as Nottingham people might put it, "as rowdy as oat." This pub had two not three separate rooms, though the spaciousness of the public bar suggested it too had suffered the 'two knocked into one' syndrome. Generations of drinkers were now growing up to sup in large vacuous spaces, the walls often lined with telly screens, while the culture of the 'snug', the kind of small room a person could go to forget and be forgotten, has passed into oblivion.

The bar was not crowded. The *Three Lions* disco belted out loud ska music in front of a giant English flag with the slogan 'For England and St George'.

Customers were a mixed crowd of young black and white, the black men weighed down with bling. Everyone was standing, and everyone shouted and gesticulated to counter the high decibel music. There were a lot of six-footers, a lot of big muscles, a lot of tattoos. But enough about the barmaids.

One barmaid served me with a bottle of Corona, then said, "Sorry, me duck, wuv run aht o' lime." "That's alright," I said, "I've brought my own." At the production from my bag of a lime fruit, the barmaid looked unsure. Was she in the presence of someone showing real prescience, prepared for any eventuality, or some sad old git with nothing better do than fill his bag with limes?

A middle-aged woman stood up and sang a slurred version of a Tom Jones song.

"D'ye lahk that, me duck?" she asked.

"Wonderful," I said. I'd hardly listened.

'Wha didn't ye clap then?" she retorted.

Behind the bar was a sign, *Cobs £1.00*, which would be meaningless information to 95 per cent of the UK population.

For the last drink I walked the length of the estate down Danethorpe Vale to The Five Ways. There was an

107

edgy sense to the pub that night, a birthday party in the big lounge with many of the guests pretty bladdered. A group of youths, twenty-something with shaved heads and tattoos were clustered in the corridor, giving it lots of lip. When I walked in, this manifestation of an ageing hippy produced some loud "ooooh!" noises.

Most of the talk was about who had been fighting who recently, and who was likely to be 'slapped' or 'battered' next. At one stage a yoof shot behind the bar and nicked a packet of crisps off the display. John the barman, who missed little, kept his nerve and demanded payment. He seemed to know the yoofs which was reassuring. The yoofs gave me various glances, but I decided against eyeballing them. I ordered a bottle of Corona, my trigger finger twitching by the lime fruits in my bag, ready for my moment of triumph.

"Got sum limes, nah," said John, and somehow I felt cheated.

THIS NOTTINGHAM
The actor Brian Blessed travelled to Nottingham to support the campaign to stop the government banning electronic collars for pets. "They just give pets a little tickle round their neck, which is better than being run over," said Blessed.

SUNDAY MAY 1

FOOD FOR FOXES
AND CLERICAL BRASSES

Derrick let slip an amazing fact. His father had fought in the First World War, at the Battle of Mons, the first major engagement between British and German troops on the Western Front in 1914. I quizzed him more about this. Derrick was just slightly younger than me. Surely he meant his grandfather?

No, it was his father. He had a memory of his father washing himself in a local stream when he, Derrick, was just a young boy. "'E must hev bin in 'is 60s or 70s then," he said. Did he want to elaborate? He was vague on detail, but then in such family matters so was I.

Much of my own family history, especially on the Mortimer side, was a series of vague shapes and images, half-known facts, unpieced together fragments. My father served in the Royal Signals during the war (the second one, by the way), much of the time in Dover. As far as I know, he was not involved in overseas combat. I didn't know much else. As a family we rarely spoke about such things, and I had never been moved to delve into the family tree. I had friends aware of the smallest minutiae of their parents', and relatives', history. This did not happen with the Mortimers.

There was an ancillary reason why Nottingham was making me feel old. The experience of being here continually caused me to visit the past, increasingly the only safe territory for old people to inhabit. I was afraid that the past might come to have too big a hold on me, at which moment I would I know I was old. This was probably paranoia, but so be it.

For the second time I cycled up to call on Helen, who lived with her Jack Russell, Sky, at 1 Danethorpe Vale, the house of the foundation stone. I was drawn back to Helen, curious about her mix of wariness towards strangers and desire for human contact, so that each time I visited, she was reluctant to let me across the threshold, but seemingly in no hurry to send me packing. I stood and chatted for forty-five minutes on the doorstep in the warm spring sunshine, Sky running in and out of my legs and round the small garden. Like many people who spend a lot of time alone, Helen talked a lot.

She was sixty-nine years old, small, birdlike and frail, and I never felt right about asking her surname. She had lived on Sherwood Estate for fifty years and was the same age when she moved here as I was when I left. So the age of nineteen was the start of her life on this estate, and the end of mine. The more I considered this, the stranger it appeared.

"I haven't been out for several weeks," she said. "I get terrible pains in the legs and I've been to the doctors and the Queens Medical Centre, and they tell me I've got a viral infection and a chest infection, and someone mentioned sciatica and maybe arthritis. They've given me a lot of pills but I don't think many of them do me much good.

My brother calls once a day from Woodthorpe. I never married and have no children. I think this estate is very quiet now. I stare out the window a lot and when people ask me why I do it, I say it's to see if there are people standing talking on the street corners, but it hardly happens now. It used to happen much more.

Helen mentioned the difficulties of having a bath. "I had a stool to sit on, and it had suction pads on the legs to keep it from moving about. I must have taken them off for some reason and now no-one can find them."

I asked Helen if she would like me to look for some more suction pads in Wilkinsons.

"Would you do that? That would be very good, thank you."

Sky was enjoying his scampering exercise. The dog probably got out very little. All the time we talked, Helen was

110

half-positioned behind the door, as if behind a safety barrier. I tried to think of her at the age of nineteen, a fresh-faced lass moving onto this estate, her life ahead of her. The imagination failed. The tunnel stretched too far back.

Helen, I realised, was but two years older than me.

A drive out for Sunday lunch was part of Valerie and Derrick's weekend, and today's trip, on which I was again invited, was a slightly shorter odyssey than the Matlock Baths expedition. We drove off along the boulevards to the Bardills Garden Centre in Stapleford. Not many people realise Nottingham has a network of boulevards: Lenton, Middleton, Gregory, Western, Radford, and Castle Boulevard. Most people associated boulevards with the French capital. Not when you grew up here in the 1950s. I clearly recall one lad in a geography lesson exclaiming, "Blahmey! Ya mean thuv got boulevards in Paris an all!"

Garden Centres are wonderful institutions for encouraging the human race's awareness of and involvement in the natural world. But they usually depress me, as most of the customers look glum and solidified.

The café was like a school canteen with serried rows of tables. Sunday roast was served from a carvery by a chef whose tinny radio sounded out at his side. After we ate Derrick got up and moved around the tables asking people for their leftovers which he wrapped up in napkins. "He used to tell them it was for the foxes, but people didn't like the idea we were feeding foxes, so now he tells them it's for the dog," said Valerie. "We don't have a dog though. It's for the foxes." Derrick returned with a large supply of meat, wrapped in a napkin.

This was another glorious day, and on our return Valerie and Derrick repaired to their splendid rear garden, where they busied themselves building their new pond. And of course, feeding the foxes.

Gardening was not for me so I jumped on my bike for a two-hour pilgrimage. I needed to visit as many past locations as possible. Often I was reluctant, as such visits proved disturbing, but it was essential.

111

From his early years, I had brought my son Dylan on trips back to Nottingham, though these had fallen off since both his Mortimer grandparents died. There was one place that Dylan had made his own in Sherwood, that belonged to his, more than his father's history. Since leaving the city I'd returned as often as possible for the October Goose Fair, held on the large stretch of open land in the north of the city called The Forest. Goose Fair was part of any Nottingham native's culture and upbringing. It was claimed by the city as the largest travelling fair in Europe, a boast curiously made by only one other competitor, Newcastle's fair, The Hoppings, held in June. When living in Sheffield, then London, then Tyneside, I would make the annual weekend pilgrimage, often bringing with me mates who I was keen to impress with this wondrous yearly extravaganza.

During these Goose Fair visits, Dylan became fascinated by a giant conker tree in Woodthorpe Park. The tree was so high and its foliage so dense that not one chink of light could be seen from beneath. Dylan immediately shinned up the lower branches and within minutes disappeared into the high density, swallowed whole by this arboreal giant. Soon there was a rustling, falling sound as he shook free the conkers, descending in such profusion that I'd need to stand clear. For thirty minutes Dylan would be up there, invisible, exploring a place as unfamiliar to most of us as the moon surface, and each year he would coax from the tree enough conkers to fill two large plastic bags. For reasons never quite understood, these conkers were a good fifty per cent bigger than those gathered on Tyneside. They were big and beautiful and as darkly shiny as well-polished furniture. The act of gently prising a conker from its spiky protective surround revealing that beautifully finished veneer remains among life's most satisfying moments. Armed with these magnificent specimens, Dylan became something of a conker celebrity at his Tyneside school.

The conker tree belonged to his own small slice of

112

Nottingham past, so that to stand under it this day evoked not my own childhood, but that of Dylan. The tree, if you'll excuse the pun, was firmly rooted in Nottingham, but via a different generation. Much of my own experience seemed isolated in time and space, beyond my reach. Not so this conker tree. Somewhere, rattling round in a sock drawer, I had examples of the tree's mega-conkers The tree was a living thing, in different senses of the word.

I photographed it and immediately texted Dylan, "Under the conker tree!"

After that I cycled the half mile down Mansfield Road to the Thackeray's Lane junction, close to which was the Church of the Good Shepherd. This had been rebuilt in

The giant horse-chestnut in Woodthorpe Park

113

1964, more or less simultaneously with my leaving Nottingham, the modern bold clean-cut concrete architecture much removed from the somewhat humble red-brick affair of my childhood, when this church had cast a long shadow.

The Leddys (my mother's family) were traditional church-going Catholic ruralites in County Cavan, Ireland. My mother brought the faith across the sea with her, and the Good Shepherd was our church, also that of her younger brother Willy, who followed his sister from Cavan a few years later. Willy married an Irish Catholic, became a Nottingham bus conductor and their family remained devout. He was active in the Nottingham Irish Centre. For the Mortimers, the faith and sense of Irishness slowly weakened, mainly through the influence of my father. He was never keen on church-going, and our own attendances began to fall away year by year. The church in those days was keen to retain its flock and I recall the visits to the Danethorpe Vale house of the priest, Father Mooney. He had a waxen shiny face and a wide frozen smile, both of which put me in mind of Archie Andrews, the 1950s' dummy of the ventriloquist Peter Brough. Few people now could even identify their local priest or vicar.

The priest's paternalistic visits would be prompted by our erratic attendance at Sunday mass. These omissions, at first infrequent, become more regular. Initially a visit from Father Mooney was sufficient to prod us back to attending, if only from fear, but this influence was waning, a trend symbolised by one particular visit. It was probably his last.

My mother, Alex and I were engaged in the fortnightly ritual of cleaning the brasses. Such ornaments are now rarely seen, and were copper not brass, but in houses on Sherwood Estate then they were almost *de rigueur*. We had around twenty examples dotted round the living room, from horse heads to Aladdin lamps to ornate ashtrays, to wall hangings mounted on long leather

114

straps. Over two weeks these ornaments would take on a tarnished appearance, to be rejuvenated by that small miracle called Duraglit. Duraglit was a pink wadding of almost cloudlike appearance. Once you removed the lid, the tin emitted a pungent carbolic odour. You ripped off part of a cloud with which you rubbed the ornament. This transferred the cloudiness to the surface of the ornament itself, and the wadding became jet back as if to emphasise how much muck had been removed. Rubbing with a clean cloth then produced an immediate transformation, as the cloudiness metamorphosed into a brilliantly gleaming shine in which you beheld your own satisfied reflection.

On this occasion we were mid-cleaning when Father Mooney called. He sat down, made some small talk and, before launching into his admonishment for our church non-attendance, politely enquired whether he could help. My mother ripped of a piece of pink Duraglit wadding and handed it to him, along with an ornament. I remember that fixed grin being lightly skew-whiff as he rubbed vigorously, and with each rub not only did the copper tarnish lessen, but so too the sense of ecclesiastical authority and influence.

In 2011, outside of services many churches are now locked and secured against thieves. The Good Shepherd was open that day and I went inside. The modern use of stained glass and the circular shape reminded me of Liverpool Catholic Cathedral, though on a much smaller scale. I sat quietly in a pew, the only person present.

Despite the family having slowly drifted away, this was still the church used for the funeral ceremony for my father in 2001, and my mother in 2008.

I was approached by the parish priest for the last 18 months, Father John Sherrington. People sitting silently in a church was once a common sight, these days less so, which explained the slight concern in Father Sherrington's voice when he enquired "Are you alright?" as if here were possibly someone about to confess to suicidal intent.

115

I told him about the brace of funerals, the family history with the church, though I declined to mention the cleaning of the brasses. We chatted in harmless fashion for a few moments. I mentioned Father Mooney, but the name meant nothing to him.

This would probably be the last ever time I would enter the building, a symbolic closing of a chapter. All human traces of my ever having lived in Nottingham seemed to have gone, and a sudden loneliness swept over me in that church.

Get up, I thought. Get off. And write your book.

MONDAY MAY 2

BURYING THE PAST AND OFF
TO THE GHOST TOWN

"Ye mate's dead," said Derrick as I came downstairs at 9am after two hours of writing.

"Who's that then?"

"Osama Bin Laden," and he laughed out loud. Me too.

I entered the living room and for the first time found a third party there.

"This is our neighbour, Verne," said Valerie, "Him and Derrick have known each other since school."

Outside of my brother, I was in touch with no-one in the world who fitted that description. Possibly scattered round the estate were individuals I would vaguely recall from Seely, Haydn Road or High Pavement Schools, but I had as little appetite to unearth them as I did to go on the Friends Reunited website. Both seemed unnatural pursuits.

Dave Coot once fitted the bill. He lived up the hill on Montfort Crescent. From the age of five, when we first met on the estate, until my late 40s, I was regularly in touch with him. Through most of our childhood we were as thick as thieves. Actually on our visits to the Sherwood Woolworths, like most kids, we often *were* thieves. Even when he and his wife Chris went to live in first Jersey and then Canada there was a link. Ironically it was after he returned to the Nottingham area that the link, for reasons never quite understood, grew weaker.

Coot, as we affectionately called him, was, and presumably still is, a large, generous person with a keen sense of humour. He failed the 11-plus, and went to Claremont Secondary Modern School, while my brother and I attended High Pavement Grammar. Even that dramatic educational schism failed to break the links. He became a

117

joiner with the now defunct Nottingham building firm Thomas Fish & Sons and still lived on the estate after the Mortimer family moved off to climb the social scale.

My father cut most of his links with Sherwood Estate once we'd removed ourselves to the posh house in Redhill, seeking contacts more on the golf course and in the business fraternity. He would often urge me to do the same, part of his paternal desire to see me succeed. Despite this move up the social ladder, neither he nor my mother showed anything but continuing warmth and friendship towards Coot.

Where was Coot now? I still had the couple's address and phone number at Bottesford on the Notts/Lincs border, where I'd visited till the mid-90s. After this, I'd heard nothing, despite enquiries and invitations. In recent days I'd left two phone messages but with no response. I considered driving the twenty miles to Bottesford, but something held me back. The couple were either (a) not now there, in which case it would be a wasted journey or (b) had chosen for some reason not to answer my phone messages, and hence were not keen to see me. All of which was a bit hyper-logical, and had I been in a different frame of mind, had my relationship with the past not been in such flux, I may well have jumped in the car, driven the twenty miles and found out what was what. But I didn't. I stayed away.

Also in the past was Friday August 9, 2002, when the front page headline in the *Nottingham Post* was *Under Siege!* highlighting how blighted was the quarter-mile shopping stretch of Mansfield Road, Sherwood. In six months there had been forty-five incidents of ram raids, armed robberies and breaking and entering. The City of Nottingham itself had an unenviable reputation at that time, hence the title of the short story collection featuring Nottingham-born writers (including me), *City of Crime* (Five Leaves Publications), a title viewed somewhat ambivalently by the local dignitaries who attended a big city centre launch at the Council House.

Since that time matters had improved for Sherwood, according to Bob Huskinson, the webmaster for the local Neighbourhood Watch branch. The phrase 'webmaster' had an exotic sense to it, almost like a Batman villain, though Bob, who brought up that August 2002 front page headline on his computer screen, was colourful without the need to be villainous. Things had improved in Sherwood, and crime had fallen, partly down to the Neighbourhood Watch efforts, partly, Bob told me, down to the CCTV cameras the Watch operated, partly down to Sherwood's new police station. To which I'd add the new street market, the new Sherwood Festival, and the colourful examples of street art.

Bob was pretty unique on Sherwood Estate, in that he invited me into his house, the first occasion I had crossed any estate threshold other than that of Derrick and Valerie.

Over a cup of tea I chatted to him and his wife Viv in the bohemian clutter of their Kneeton Close home, where he was keen to emphasise Neighbourhood Watch was not just a cranky group of curtain-twitchers, but a grass roots positive force of which David Cameron's Big Society should be proud, just as he was obviously proud of his own efforts.

That evening I took a bus ride down to the city centre. The Royal Wedding, plus two back-to-back Bank Holiday weekends, had left the nation exhausted and hung-over from an excess of leisure, making this particular evening one of the quietest of the year. The Market Square was eerily empty, as were the surrounding streets, a silence broken only by the ghostly sound of a single, unseen busker's wailing voice.

On the corner of Exchange Walk, facing onto Market Square, sat the Smiths branch of NatWest Bank, In superficial appearance it was little different to 1960, though then called National Provincial, when as a fresh-faced lad of seventeen, I was escorted by my father to meet the manager and open my very first bank account.

119

This may not quite have been the time of frock-coats, quill pens, and clerks in wing collars perched on high stools, but it was still a world removed from banking 2011-style. My account was opened in a ledger the size of a football pitch, using a fountain pen rather than a quill, and I knew instinctively I was in safe hands. Though a bank may have been a fairly dull institution, it was also caring, paternalistic, cautious, wise. A bank was knowledgeable about money management in a way we mere mortals were not. We offered ourselves to its welcoming bosom knowing that a bank would as soon betray its customers as a mother would poison her own child. And the bank manager's face was almost as familiar to customers as that of the doctor, or the milkman.

I was never quite sure when it began to go wrong, or when bankers began to lose our trust, to slide down that long slippery slope by the base of which, despite millions spent on clever advertising and marketing campaigns, they became among the most reviled members of our society, heartless, parasitical, exploitative, and trousering shamefully huge bonuses at a time when the poorer members of society were denied basic health and living facilities. Bankers competed in the popularity stakes with the likes of Rupert Murdoch.

Personally, I put the moment of decline down to an advertising campaign that showed a local branch manager emerging from a wardrobe. Doctors and milkmen never needed to emerge from our wardrobes to prove their accessibility. These days I had as much chance of meeting my bank manager, and I use the possessive 'my' suggesting some kind of personal link that does not exist, as I had of meeting Madonna. But at least I knew what Madonna looked like, and could hear her sing.

I walked up into the Lace Market, a distinctive city centre area, home to the once flourishing but now almost defunct Nottingham lace industry. Much of this was still a commercial district, a mini City of London whose main bustle was in business hours. But there were also pubs

120

and restaurants and clubs. Gone was my favourite pub The Dog & Bear, and the newer variety of watering hole went for single word names, such as Cape or Image, or the ultra-swish Tantra, open till 3am, with its red carpet entrance and strict dress code, a sense of sophistication slightly belied by the misspelt publicity outside, with its claim to be *Impossibly Glamourous* [sic].

One traditional corner pub just re-opened and restored to its former glory was the Thurland Hall, with its cursive gilt sign and ornate acid-etched windows. Inside, the décor was stained wood and period lighting, and on this evening it hosted only four people, including me, the barman and the DJ, the last of whom happily, given his meagre audience, kept a low and quiet profile. In the days of my Nottingham drinking apprenticeship, the short thoroughfare of Clumber Street boasted three hostelries. The Corner Pin had gone, as had The Crystal Palace, though the distinctive gold ormolu décor and green tiles of the Lion Hotel, plus the fine curved window, were still in evidence. A pity the pub wasn't. The façade was a sleight of hand, a *trompe l'oeil*. The premises were now owned by Sun Valley Amusements, and the interior boasted not Home Ales, a name still etched into that same curved window, but slot machines and bandits.

Home Ales was brewed by Home Brewery, one of the three independent Nottingham breweries, all of whom were swallowed by large corporate competitors with assurances of future viability, and shortly thereafter closed down.

The Home Brewery's distinctive Arnold premises, complete with the beautiful long frieze of Bacchanalian indulgences, had been saved and was now used by Notts County Council. The metal sign HOME OF THE BEST ALES had been incorporated with the county logo, which naturally included the Major Oak. The final word had been removed. Quite neat really.

Also gone was Shipstone's, though here too their magnificent Old Basford Brewery had been saved. A Shippo's pub trademark was an illuminated red star

121

which was so lovely Lenin nicked it for the Soviet Union. The pungent malty smell which wafted from that brewery into my old High Pavement School in Stanley Street will never quite leave my nostrils. The main Shippo's drink was known locally as 'fayting bitter', it having been statistically proved that more fights broke out at closing time outside Shippo's pub than any other brewery.

The third Nottingham brewery of my youth, now also gone, was Hardy Hanson Kimberley Ales. Having said which, the city does now boast a healthy number of micro-breweries.

Three pubs on nearby Parliament Street had survived the years. The Coach and Horses was now a high decibel joint, its crowded and animated interior like a moving tableau seen through the large front window. The Blue Bell, its distinctive eponymous feature hanging outside, was more laid back, less in your face, while the Turf Tavern, despite its fluorescent sign blazing forth, was a late-night venue, its doors still shuttered mid-evening.

Round the corner was the city's new drinking strip on Forman Street, where cafés, bars and music spilled onto the pedestrianised street. On weekend nights here you were unlikely to meet anyone over the age of 25, apart from me, that is.

As I waited for the return bus on Sherwood Street, a curious incident happened. Siren blaring, blue light flashing, a police car screamed past and whizzed through the red traffic light at the Shakespeare Street junction. In 1962 a similar incident involving a police car and shooting the lights occurred at this same junction. Except it was me that shot the lights. And the vehicle I hit was the police car.

I had only recently passed the driving test, and was still on what was known as 'the pink slip'. I received a hefty fine, with three points on my licence before I'd even got it.

Thus began the slow realisation that I was not a good driver, a confession that few males ever make. Painful

122

though this realisation initially was, it later freed me from all manner of macho expectations including any desire to talk clutch systems, or watch such nonsense as *Top Gear*.

My destination for a final drink was The Five Ways where I arrived at 10pm to find the place, for the first time ever in my experience, closed and shuttered during opening hours. I stared at the dark and noiseless pub. Had the financial burden of buying lime fruits for Mortimer proved too heavy? Had too many packets of crisps been nicked?

Such frippery apart, this was an epiphany moment, the moment when this watering hole, such a vital part of my upbringing, really began to emerge from its sepia-tinted past into its harsher, monochrome present.

THIS NOTTINGHAM

A Nottingham city farm in St Anns has recaptured one of its birds after it wandered into a city centre bank. Stonebridge City Farm were contacted by the bank after the red rosella walked into the premises near the Market Square.

TUESDAY MAY 3

TWO WHEELS GOOD,
AND PLACES OF NO RETURN

Breakfast routine was now well-established at number 85. I would flounce downstairs in my black silk kimono at 9am, pick up the small tray set for me by Valerie, sit down in front of the telly and tuck into the bowl of porridge and pumpkin seeds, exchanging a few comments with Valerie and Derrick, each similarly armed with a breakfast tray. Thus we three sat, paying homage to the breakfast god of daytime TV, offering the occasional comment on the minor celebs or telly chefs on view. The cultural transition, after two hours of writing and yoga, was a strange one.

Danethorpe Vale stretches more than half a mile from the estate's base at Valley Road to the summit, where it meets Magnus Road and Mansfield Road. If not quite of Sisyphean proportions, the hill is steep enough to slowly sap the energy of a cyclist, leaving him or her well puffed at the top. I resisted the strong temptation to dismount for the final slope, a decision leaving me both knackered and triumphant. Slowly my black bike had become a part of me. It couldn't match the molecular exchange of machine and human known to Flann O'Brien's *Third Policeman*, but there was still that satisfying sense of a vehicle whose energy source was one hundred per cent human, without recourse to internal combustion engines or fossil fuels. Some years since, the bike had been voted the world's best ever invention, and it could well be the saviour of the human race.

Small running repairs were required this morning. After climbing Danethorpe Vale, I decided to cycle back to the Arnold bike shop to buy a bracket for a back mudguard which was rattling like a loose denture. The journey

124

allowed me to compare two verbally similar but artistically very different signs. In Sherwood on Mansfield Road was an eye-catching and original *Welcome to Sherwood* sign made by local artists Sophie Robbins and Rachel Ainley. The duo had won a recent Grab a Grand award for an artistic venture based in Sherwood. Positioned on the wide pavement, it was two-sided, the words in a distinctive red freestyle, the board garlanded with a whole cluster of inlaid ceramic leaves, each leaf giving some visual reference to an aspect of the area and the city. My only complaint was that for the best pedestrian impact, it should have been turned through 90 degrees.

Outside the new Sainsbury's in Arnold was a *Welcome to Arnold* sign, obviously created by the supermarket giant itself. It was in the company's colours, artistically barren with a dull sense of corporate functionality.

I spotted a further example of individual flair when, mudguard secured, I cycled back up Mansfield Road to Sherwood. Just before Woodthorpe Drive, outside Pete's Barbers' Shop, stood a full-sized dummy of Batman,

The eye-catching "Welcome to Sherwood" sign

The less than eye-catching "Welcome to Arnold" sign

round his neck a sign with the entreaty, *Haircut, Sir?* The dummy changes its clothes more often than most humans.

I couldn't quite imagine such eccentricity outside Sainsbury's or Tesco.

Never once, in my previous Nottingham existence, had I cycled from Sherwood into the city centre. I'd ridden push-bikes in my early years, though journeying the busy road south into Nottingham was considered far too dangerous a journey for a young lad. The roads were now ten times busier, but unlike some cyclists I felt no fear whizzing through traffic on two wheels.

En route to the city centre I called at the Forest Recreation area which each year hosted the famous Goose Fair. So strong were the Goose Fair associations with this place that to cycle along Gregory Boulevard even on this bright and warm sunny day evoked dank October evenings and the rank but intoxicating smell of hot dogs and onions. In my ears were the strident whinings of the rides, the blare of the music, the screams of the girls twirled fast on the waltzers, the throb of the generators, the barking invitations from the sideshow owners to view the flea circus, Scotland's tallest man or the two-headed lady. I could taste those pink clouds of candy floss, which were magicked up by dipping a stick into a mysterious whooshing drum to whose inner perimeter clung what seemed like trembling cobwebs, or ghostly fibres, which rapidly shrank to sticky tar in the mouth.

The Forest *was* Goose Fair to me, and for me to view it at any other time or in any other context was rare. This may explain how little I had previously been aware of its bowling and putting greens, its cemetery and cricket pitch, its pleasant tree-lined paths rising up to Forest Road. From here you could descend Waverley Street to discover another arboreal wonder, the Arboretum, on whose lovely lawns office workers would stretch and sunbathe their lunchtime away. Later in the day I would be in the quiet calm of Nottingham Castle gardens, and realise just what a green city I had been born into.

The Goose Fair site was within the much larger overall area of The Forest, and was used the rest of the year for car parking. Opposite this site was once Manning School, the sister school to High Pavement. I had vivid memories of Manning, particularly the girl pupils' short red and white gingham skirts whose flimsy nature saw them blow high in the wind, providing Mortimer with some of his earliest erotic memories. One bonus of being a Manning pupil was that you were given Goose Fair Friday as a holiday, the noise of the nearby fairground considered too much a distraction to academic learning.

Manning had gone, in its place a piece of brutalist architecture, the Djanogly City Academy, the Djanoglys being one of the leading Nottingham manufacturing families with whom I remember my father had some dealings, not particularly to his own advantage. The young Djanogly these days cuts a dash as a Conservative MP.

I walked into the Academy and asked the young woman at reception if present students were allowed the same Goose Fair privilege. "It did happen the year the academy opened in 2006," she said, "But not since then." Thus the decline of the educational system...

I now set off for my final mile's bike journey to the city centre. Think of most continental cities where great legions of bikes are parked up in the centre, then think of our own major conurbations where the odd machine might be locked to a lamp-post. Most people in the UK do not own a bike and if they did, would view tackling city centre traffic on two engineless wheels as some kind of nightmare. London's ambitious bike hire system was making some inroads into our resistance, but urban bike converts were still few.

I was one of them. Not just a convert, but a zealot. Cycling in city centres choked with traffic bestowed an exhilarating freedom denied to those locked in their metal containers. The pure delight of whizzing past the jams of stationary cars, darting between the frustrated and gridlocked motorists, the sheer sense of anarchy to be free of the self-imposed constraints of the motorist was intoxicating. These motorists were sealed in metal and glass. They nudged forwards inches at a time. Their vain search for a parking space saw them endlessly circling the same streets. And they were shut off from the world. Me? I was the nimble flea among the slow-moving elephants. I skedaddled and skidoodled along this street and that. I could dismount and nip up a one-way street for a short cut. I could squeeze through the narrowest of gaps. I could jump off on impulse to view an interesting shop window display. I could eavesdrop on the conversations of the people I cycled past. Parking restrictions, traffic wardens — such things were irrelevant to me.

Thus to Nottingham Castle! This wasn't really a castle at all, though it had once been. In the Middle Ages Nottingham could boast one of the country's finest genuine castles, a highly impressive and dominating location perched on its outcrop of rock, surveying all before it. But in 1651 after the Civil War it was mainly demolished, and not rebuilt for another two and a half centuries, so what we now had perched on that rock was an early 20th century apology for a castle. Reconstructed in 1908, it was pleasant enough, but had more the soft architectural lines of a country house than the muscle-bound stance of a castle.

Like the Major Oak, Nottingham Castle with its Robin Hood associations was a vital part of the city's cultural heritage and tourism industry. It had also featured on the inside flap of Players cigarette packets (Players being a Nottingham born company). It was now a museum and coffee house, set within beautifully landscaped gardens, an oasis of calm sealed and secured high up above the tumult of the city. On such a balmy day, the temptation to stretch out on the manicured lawns was irresistible. Entrance, once free, was now a fiver, though the friendly man on the turnstile asked, "Why not bring your bike inside?" which would never have happened had I been driving a Fiat Uno.

Nottingham Castle was also home to Mortimer's Hole. To be born in Nottingham with the surname Mortimer was unfortunate, and, as a child, led to the kind of unsavoury ribbings of which the Johnstons and Taylors of this world were blissfully ignorant.

Here's the story. Roger Mortimer, Earl of March, murdered King Edward II in 1327 and illegally took not only the crown, but also the King's wife Isabella. Mortimer ruled England for three years until in 1330 supporters of Isabella's son (who became Edward III) used an escape tunnel (or 'counter-attack' tunnel as it was known in the castle), to break into the King Regent's bed-chamber and capture him and Isabella between the sheets — what a tabloid story! Mortimer was hanged, Isabella imprisoned, and should you wish to learn more, try the book *England's Greatest Traitor* by Ian Mortimer, one of Roger's descendants, and, judging by the book title, showing scant family loyalty.

Even the most illiterate of youths in Nottingham knew of Mortimer's Hole, for thus was the tunnel there-after named, and its entrance is prominently displayed and named in the castle grounds. I was constantly targeted by contemporaries, who felt upon hearing my surname, that the height of comic originality was to point a finger and screech *Mortimer's Hole!* unaware I had heard this anal jibe twenty times before, probably that month.

Mortimer's Hole is mentioned, incidentally, in Alan Sillitoe's novel *Saturday Night and Sunday Morning,* where the anti-hero Arthur Seaton is disparaging about it, though with less reason than I have.

Nottingham, built on bunter sandstone, is riddled with similar caves and tunnels. One of the city's present-day novelists, David Belbin, uses these to good effect in his latest book, the highly readable political thriller *Bone and Cane* (Tindal Street Press), where a main character grows a subterranean forest of dope plants in the caves below the well-to-do city centre area, The Park, built by 19th century wealthy lace manufacturers.

Talking of new books, that day's edition of the *Nottingham Post* featured a review of the latest publica-tion in the Robin Hood industry. *Robin Hood*, by J.C. Holt (Thames & Hudson) was the result of thirty years research, and suggested that not only Sherwood but also Barnsdale in South Yorkshire were Robin Hood's centres of operations. I'd never been to Barnsdale, in fact I'd never heard of it, but I suspected there were few statues of our folk hero there, and marketing-wise they'd have a long way to catch up.

That evening, a small revelation. When studying a map of Nottinghamshire, I came across the village of Kneeton for the first time. Further map probings revealed other familiar estate names. Had I not realised, asked Valerie, that all Sherwood Estate thoroughfares were named after Nottinghamshire villages? To my shame I had not. We lads rarely ventured into the county itself. And

Nottinghamshire was still much less-known territory to me than many other counties in England.

I *had* known the interior of number 97 Danethorpe Vale, my home from the age of three to nineteen. I had no memories of previous family locations. Like first love, your first real home, though not necessarily the most important, was unique. Through infancy, to boyhood, to youth, to teenager, to manhood, and all within those same four walls.

Had I become obsessed about entering that house? Probably. I talked to Valerie and Derrick about calling on Derrick Junior. Why not, they said, though I may get no reply. I armed myself with a four-pack of Corona Beer, for which of course I had ample supplies of lime. I covered the short distance from number 85 to 97. I walked up that oh-so-familiar, yet alien front path with an acute nervousness that almost stopped me dead. The garden was now overrun. In the long grass were two abandoned chairs, three wheelie bins, a thrown-out suitcase and various other pieces of detritus. The hedge soared skywards, blinds were drawn on the front downstairs window, the glass upstairs was cracked. The front door was in a sorry state, the faded paint chipped and peeling, the number 97 worse for wear. A small metal St George's flag was next to the house number. There was no bell. I gave a couple of short raps on the knocker. The sound rang hollow inside the fabled house. No response. I knocked again. Same. I shouted "Hello!' through the raised letter-flap, and felt slightly ridiculous. I walked up through the communal 'entry' dividing numbers 97 and 99. Bathrooms had been downstairs in these houses, situated off the kitchen, an inconvenience meaning post-bathing you had to rush dripping wet through the living room to get upstairs. I was always unsure who was the more embarrassed at such times, myself or any visitors who were innocently drinking a cup of tea.

The frosted bathroom windows still stared across the 'entry' at one another, though I assumed all the estate houses now had upstairs ablutions and that these one-time bathrooms were used for different purposes. There was no longer a rear entrance to number 97. The one-time gate had been replaced by a high solid fence that blocked out even the merest glimpse of that garden which had been a childhood universe.

I viewed this tall blank barrier like a Palestinian seeing for the first time the Israeli Wall in the West Bank, except that wall excluded the Palestinians from their day-to-day present. I was only denied the past.

My instinct told me that Derrick was inside the house, but also that he had no intention of putting in an appearance. I turned away from the high fence, and carrying my four-pack of Corona, walked back down the 'entry' and along the dishevelled path. Once through the gate, I turned to look again at the dismal house front. Inside me was a huge sadness, also disappointment, also confusion. Also, to be honest, slight relief not to be called upon to confront whatever lay beyond that bleak-looking front door.

That evening The Five Ways had reopened. My enquiries elicited from John the information that business had been so dreadful the previous evening, they'd simply shut up shop. This was a big pub, expensive to maintain. How many closed nights could they afford?

Meantime, The Five Ways Lime Fruits Saga was set to continue. "Do you have any lime yet?" I asked John.

He replied, "'Ar."

"Then I'll have a bottle of Sol with a slice of lime," I said. He brought the drink, plonked it down, took the money, then disappeared. Inside the neck was a slice of lemon.

I looked up for John but he had been replaced by the barmaid, Zoe. I asked her, "Can I have a slice of lime with this please?"

"Ent got no limes," said Zoe.

"Here," I said and handed over a lime fruit. "Take a slice off that. You can keep the rest."

In theory the pub should have been busy that evening. Jazz Night was in the concert room, bingo in another room, and there were also sessions of the skill-free card game Sticky 13s. But the concert room was sparsely populated, and fewer than a dozen people were playing bingo.

I was becoming invisible in The Five Ways. The more I visited the more anonymous I became. For a gregarious person for whom acceptability was important, this was disturbing. Early communication had vanished. I had seen no sign recently of the proprietors Steve and Yvette. My tentative ventures at communication felt increasingly strained, and produced at best monosyllabic responses.

So that the main emotion generated now by my visits was one of loneliness. Yet even as I stood alone that night in the corridor, something changed, a realisation that my ambitions in returning to this one-time haunt had been misguided, a belief I would simply walk through the door and be accepted. There was no way a ghost could properly be accepted. Which is what I was here. A ghost. My time for The Five Ways had been decades ago. Now, for better or for worse, was the time for other people.

And like a ghost, I became a detached observer, an entity from another dimension, amorphously drifting among those few people for whom The Five Ways in 2011 was a reality. At 11.30pm the jazz players, grey-haired elderly gents, walked from the concert room with their instruments and out to the cars, presumably anticipating cocoa back home. The bingo and Sticky 13 sessions had long finished, and Carl, the regular 'corridor customer', supped his final pint of Guinness and shoved his last coins into the bandit before he too made off.

I made off as well, that short, oh-so-familiar walk from The Five Ways to the bottom of Danethorpe Vale. The pub was now more alien to me than at any time in my life.

THIS NOTTINGHAM

A Carlton man has been ordered to pay almost £800 after he was caught dropping a cigarette butt in the town. Mark Bromley was spotted by a Neighbourhood Warden, and failed to pay the initial £50 fine within 14 days.

WEDNESDAY MAY 4

THE NON-SLIP MAT
AND A PLETHORA OF SAUSAGE

Hits from the Blitz was advertised in The Sherwood Inn, which was looking for a new manager. It was the 70th anniversary of Germany pounding Nottingham's industrial infrastructure, though the latest theory was that the planes' actual targets had been Derby and they had taken a wrong turn.

The *Nottingham Post* was featuring blitz anecdotes of old-timers. This outreached even my own Nottingham memories. Not that I was writing a memoir, which was very much the current literary fashion. Visiting the past was uneasy for me, and required regular dashes back to the present for relief, hence the chronological mix of this book. Some took refuge in the past. I took it in the present.

And the present was the 97/85 Danethorpe Vale situation. The relationship between Derrick Senior, Derrick Junior and Valerie was a complex one where I had to tread warily, for there was no more dangerous minefield than the territory of other families. Derrick Junior would call briefly once or twice a day. He was skinny, angular, shaven-headed and slightly taut. He would sometimes arrive bearing sausages or a chicken which required cooking as he had no oven.

On this morning, he was after a lift to the Job Centre in Arnold to sign on. At the door I told him about my visit the previous day bearing four bottles of beer. He nodded his head but said nothing. Whenever I mentioned gaining access to his house, he shrank inwardly like a prodded snail retreating to its shell. Despite this obvious discomfort, I pushed it further. "I'll give you a lift to Arnold," I said, "if you'll let me into your house."

Derrick Junior made various indeterminate noises all of which suggested a negative response and began backing down the path.

"Alright," I said, "I'll give you a lift, no strings attached."

I calculated that once I had Derrick Junior as a captive audience, my own unique milk of human kindness would be enough to melt his heart, which must be the worst mixed metaphor of the decade.

"Raht," he said, and for an unfathomable reason I felt that it was *him* doing me the favour. Conversation in the car was not easy for either of us. I asked him what he would do if his father and Valerie went ahead with a proposed move to Dorset, which would mean his father selling number 85, and him leaving the house in which he was born. He shrugged his shoulders and said nothing. I realised he was not the kind of man to indulge in the abstractions of theoretical forward planning.

He asked me what kind of place I lived in and I told him Cullercoats was an old fishing village on the north-east coast.

"Posh then," he said. It isn't.

Not many more words were exchanged before I dropped Derrick Junior off at the centre.

One hope had been that either Derrick Senior or Valerie might take Derrick Junior to one side and say, "Why not just let Peter into the house, eh?"

The family dynamics, I realised, simply did not operate in that way. It would not happen.

"The thing is," said Valerie, a woman blessed with the gift of always seeing the positive in people, "he can be such a lovely lad." She was right. I found Derrick Junior likeable. If only he'd let me in his damned house.

The second Sherwood Estate house where I got to the door but no further was Helen's, at the top of Danethorpe Vale. I'd made enquiries about suction pads for the chair to be used in Helen's bath, but to no avail. Instead in Wilkinson's I bought a non-slip bath mat which would both cling to the bath surface and also make secure anything placed on top.

I knocked on her door and after a long wait and a good deal of excited barking from the Jack Russell, Helen opened it, emerging half-way round the frame. Again I was struck how like a nervous bird she seemed. She looked genuinely surprised when I produced the non-slip mat.

"Oh," she said, "How nice, thank you. How much do I owe you?"

"Nothing," I said. "Is your brother coming today?"

"Yes, he's coming later."

"You could ask him to fit the mat. It's very simple."

"Yes, I will, thank you."

"And I'll call back in a couple of days to check everything is OK."

"Yes, that's right."

I was now so accustomed to standing on that doorstep in the spring sunshine (and the sun had barely gone in during my Nottingham time) while Sky scampered around my legs and the garden, that to venture any further, actually to enter that house, would have seemed unnatural. I had no idea what Helen made of me. Had she remembered my previous visit, or did she simply see me as some kind of madman appearing on the doorstep with a non-slip bath mat? After a few more moments, I left.

In my bedroom at number 85 was a small bookcase containing maybe forty volumes, included in which were four *Just William* books by Richmal Crompton. William Brown was the leading literary influence of my younger years. In my Sherwood Estate childhood, I had become immersed in William's world, despite it being different to my own in almost every way. I was growing up in the 50s and 60s on an urban working-class council estate. William's childhood was the interwar years in a sleepy, very middle-class, very rural village. No matter. The irascible William did battle with a whole sequence of adult characters, some grotesque, some hilariously funny, and he always emerged on top. In *Just William* books adult-hood was seen as a slightly dotty affair whose whole philosophy and make-up were at odds with the universe as viewed by William Brown and The Outlaws. This struck such a chord with young Mortimer's view of the grown-up world that I took comfort and refuge therein. Here was something I'd never experienced in the written word. Here was an adult writer who understood perfectly the logic and superiority of childhood.

Whenever I came across a Richmal Crompton *Just William* book (I now have a full bookshelf of them at home) I would think of my three Mortimer uncles, Loo, Harry and Jack, all of whom were eccentric characters perfectly fitting the William Brown mould of adulthood.

Uncle Loo was tiny, yet had a strong and strident voice. He had not missed a Notts County game in years. I suspect he was at their opening match in 1862. He rode his small motorbike across the country to catch every Notts County fixture, the white helmet sitting like an oversized egg on his head, and on the pillion sat his young son Malcolm, who accompanied his father almost before he could walk. The last time I saw Malcolm, some years back, I realised he had metamorphosed into his father.

Within seconds of meeting Loo, he would be holding forth on the latest fortunes of County with a passion, an atten-tion to tiny detail, such as the goal differences of the four teams immediately above and below, that was oblivious to the rapidly-shrinking interest of the party addressed. Even in his later, frailer years, Loo seemed energised by the subject of Notts County. As a County fan my interest was held longer than most. The team imbued in him an evan-gelical fervour that made many of his contemporaries seem pale. The universe revolved around Meadow Lane, and no-one, not even Galileo, could prove otherwise. His wife Marge was a wee dumpling who I barely heard utter a syllable about Notts County. She and my own mother did not speak — one of those mysterious family feuds whose relevance had long since passed into antiquity, but which

138

was kept alive on some strange life support system which neither party would agree to withdraw.

Both Uncle Harry and Uncle Jack at some stage in their lives had suffered some undefined physical setback leaving both incapacitated and unable to work. Harry had a nervous twitch, and his skin was flaky and blotched. He was a thin man, given to a sudden nervous laugh, and his eyes would dart this way and that like some cornered animal, so that at times I felt he was terrified of life itself. When he spoke it was often hesitant, like an engine being half kick-started into life then dying away. Memories of his wife Sheila are hazy as she and Harry separated when I was still young. But here was a strange thing. Two months before this book was due for publication I had a letter from a certain Sheila Reid. Included with the letter was a 1947 wedding photograph from her own marriage to my Uncle Harry. And included in the wedding group (as well as the happy couple and Sheila's parents) are the four year old Peter Mortimer, the six year old Alex Mortimer, and our parents. The photo adorns the title page of this book. Sheila (who remarried) now lives in Keyworth, Notts. She had no idea the Nottingham book was due, but had written concerning another Mortimer tome. Serendipity.

Uncle Jack was equally thin, and had early on suffered some back complaint which had left him stooped. Along with the thinness, this put one in mind of a paper clip. He was also quite tall, but the angle of his spine left him looking up at you. Jack knew about hi-fi systems and records, and one image I have of him is stooping over the music system clutching a shiny black 78 disc. His small black moustache was similar to that of the keyboard player in the Dutch band *Sparks*. Jack moved slowly and his universe seemed at a different tempo. His wife Gladys was a mature painted doll whose manufactured glamour put me in mind of Bette Davis' *Baby Jane*.

These three Mortimer uncles hovered continually at the edge of my Nottingham existence. None lived on the estate, and I saw them irregularly. It was later, when reading Laurie Lee's *Cider With Rosie*, that I realised the strange exoticism of uncles was fertile ground for writers.

Compared to my uncles, my father seemed incredibly together and fully functional. I learned little of the four's upbringing, though their mother — my grandmother — was also eccentric, given to wide-brimmed veiled hats, Victorian dresses, reading tea leaves, and moving house at such regular intervals my father told me he once came home from school to find the family had upped sticks and gone. She occasionally lived on the estate, and most other parts of Nottingham too. Richmal Crompton would have been proud.

I finally got access to The Place, Sherwood's arts and community centre in Melrose Street, off the main Mansfield Road. This was converted from the bus drivers' canteen at the rear of what had once been Sherwood Bus Depot, and was now shared between Nottingham Community Transport and an impressive new Wetherspoons named The Samuel Hall. Hall was a Nottingham lace manufacturer, but also, in the early 19th century, planned out the first streets of Sherwood as it looked today.

I liked The Place. It had that creative community spirit, that grassroots atmosphere that left you feeling more optimistic about the human race. I stumbled into the middle of a yoga class, but there was also life-drawing, pilates, oil painting, pottery, creative writing, and other activities; it was like pulling back a curtain on another level of Sherwood life.

Administrator Jane Gill told me the centre was self-supporting though much aided by the City Council charging only a peppercorn annual rent of £10. While we chatted she mentioned a book called *The History of Sherwood* by Tony Fay, and ten minutes later I had dug it out from Sherwood Library's local history section.

The small detail of history is often as intriguing as major events — my excuse for including the following from the book.

140

The final film to be shown at Sherwood's Metropole Cinema (now the Co-op Supermarket) when it closed in 1973 was Lindsay Anderson's *O Lucky Man*. The cinema had opened in 1937 with the film *The Champagne Waltz* starring Victor MacLagen, who curiously was related to the Metropole's first manager.

T.E. Lawrence, he of *Lawrence of Arabia* fame, and for the more intellectual out there, the author of *Seven Pillars of Wisdom*, bought no fewer than six Brough Superior motorbikes from the Brough factory in Haydn Road, Sherwood, and the book included a photo of the famous man sat astride the sixth (presumably the one on which he crashed and died) alongside a member of the Brough family. So Nottingham had links with not one, but two famous Lawrences. End of minor history lesson.

I'd offered to cook again that evening. I made a chicken casserole flavoured with lemon served with mashed potatoes and cabbage which Derrick and Valerie ate in silence, as we sat with our perched trays and watched the six o'clock news. They'd been effusive with praise about my cheese and onion pie, so how come no commendations now?

Showing great subtlety, I asked, "Don't you like it?"

"I'll have some more," said Valerie which was praise of sorts, though maybe diplomatic. It did earn the two of them their pudding of apricot pie and custard. Custard-making was a slightly obsessive act for me, and I had been known to consider wrist-slitting were the custard found to contain even the smallest lump. Luckily not this time.

Later I considered that possibly the lemon had been seen as slightly unwelcome. I said nothing.

I'd bought the chicken at the Sherwood butchers of J.T. Beedham & Sons, which had on display the widest choice of sausage I had encountered anywhere on the globe. Their fifty-five flavours included rhubarb and also marmalade, more proof of Sherwood's growing cosmopolitan nature.

It was rare for me not to venture forth in the evening. This was the exception. After watching Man Utd batter Shalke 4–1 in the European Cup, a weariness took hold of me and I dragged myself upstairs, leaving Valerie reading my book *Broke Through Britain*. Strange that she should be working her way through one Mortimer odyssey while I was penning another.

THIS NOTTINGHAM

People from Nottingham are more likely to dress provocatively on holiday — it's the highest percentage in the UK. Some 18 per cent of Nottingham travellers do so.

THURSDAY MAY 5

ECONOMIES OF SOAP
AND THE WATERWAYS REBORN

I was aware that the kitchen at 85 Danethorpe Vale was very much Valerie's theatre of operations, and a region little frequented by Derrick. I was also aware how instinctively territorial people could be about such exclusive areas, and how shaped to their own individuality they could become. I was more domestic than Derrick, more used to pottering around the kitchen back home, cooking, washing-up, tidying. For a writer domesticity can be a vital therapy, an antidote to the act of putting words on paper. Condemned to a daily drudgery, many poor souls no doubt dream of writing a novel. In contrast, the author often needs to get cracking with the vacuum cleaner to help clear the writer's block.

I trod with care, knowing the importance of routine, knowing how in a kitchen everything had its place. I cleaned away every crumb, washed up every small plate, wiped down the draining board after me.

One particular domestic trait I recognised was Valerie's Soap Economy. Soap Economy operated like this: instead of throwing away the last sliver of a bar of soap, you attached it to the new bar. This was a skill known to my mother which she had tried to pass down to her son, but never with great success. In my own attempts the small piece of soap always somehow detached itself from the large piece of soap and to my shame I had many years since abandoned the practice.

Now I was able to study carefully Valerie's Soap Economy tactics. Rather than simply press one piece to the other, Valerie carefully smoothed the entire periphery of the small soap edges down onto the new soap, not resting until all evidence of a join had gone, and we were left with a single unit, albeit one with a slightly raised bump. Patience was required in this exercise, but patience was rewarded, as patience always is, for the two pieces thereafter were bonded for life — brief though that life would be.

Brought up in the hardships of rural Ireland, my mother had various other economy devices. She would switch off the electric iron five minutes before finishing so as not to waste heat. She encouraged us to use the edges of towels when drying, to avoid a threadbare centre. Boiling up bones for soup was regular. We were occasionally allowed the indulgence of an added tin of Heinz Cream of Tomato, though I was about thirteen years old before I sampled the sheer luxury of Heinz Cream of Tomato soup untainted by the oily presence of the boiled bones.

There was news of a planned play about Notts County to celebrate the club's 150th anniversary in 2012. Allow me my small moment of bragging to inform you that Notts County reach this landmark before any other professional club in the entire world.

The play was commissioned by Nottingham Playhouse and written by the Southwell-born author Billy Ivory, who recently adapted DH Lawrence's novel *Women in Love* for the BBC — and what greater Nottingham commendation could there be than that? Ivory's piece is based loosely on the book by the journalist/ex-Notts-County player David McVay, *Steak Diana Ross*, which evokes a 1970s' world of professional football far removed from today's pampered, bad-tempered and remote prima donnas.

In one incident, the County goalie, having let in a bagful of goals, is waiting after the game at the bus-stop near the Meadow Lane ground. Could you believe modern-day players bussing it home? He sticks out his hand and as the bus draws to a halt, the man behind him is heard to comment, "Fost bleddy thing 'e's stopped all afternoon."

Billy Ivory was one of several Nottingham dramatists commissioned by Giles Croft, artistic director of Nottingham Playhouse. A little-known play by Henrik Ibsen, *The*

League of Youth, had been adapted by Andy Barrett — who also wrote a play on the death of the Nottinghamshire coal industry — and was to open in a few days time. In the autumn there would be Michael Pinchbeck's play, *The Ashes*, about the controversial 1920s' body-line tour of Australia, where the two Nottinghamshire fast bowlers Larwood and Vose were seen as the villains of the piece. (Point of interest: a new private mini-estate next to The Five Ways included a Larwood Close.) Croft had also recently commissioned work from Nottingham playwrights Stephen Lowe, Nick Wood, and Amanda Whittington. I met the director in the Playhouse Bar where he managed a spot of impressive multi-tasking by talking eloquently about his eleven years at The Playhouse while simultaneously negotiating a wobbling fish-finger sandwich that was three storeys high.

Prior to Nottingham, Croft worked in Watford and before that as literary manager of the National Theatre. At Nottingham Playhouse his task, at a time when subsidised theatre was under all sorts of pressures, was to fill a 750-seat main auditorium. Like many other organisations, the Playhouse's Arts Council grant had been cut back — by eleven per cent. Nottingham City Council coughed up £280,000 annually of which £80,000 went straight back as rent. There was also support from the County Council.

"Things have changed in those eleven years," he told me. "Audiences have become broader, and there are new venues in the city, the New Arts Exchange, and the new Lakeside Arts Centre."

He also mentioned NEAT 11, the three week Nottingham European Arts and Theatre Festival 2011, which I would mainly miss, but for which Ibsen's aforementioned *The League of Youth* was the curtain raiser. The Brits were notoriously insular about staging European theatre (when did you last catch a production of the great German playwright Schiller for instance?) so this was a bit of a discovery; two plays by Goethe — including his mammoth and rarely performed *Faust*, a German version of Buchner's *Woyzeck* with English surtitles and music by Tom Waits, a dramatisation of Hans Christian Andersen's children's stories, Beethoven's only opera, *Fidelio*, a Polish play about football staged at the Nottingham Forest ground, street theatre from two Nottingham companies, and much more, including a show for that neglected theatre audience, the under-fours.

Giles Croft eventually won the battle with the fish finger sandwich and went off back to rehearsals. I was happy enough in the bar. Sitting round in theatres was one of the best therapies I knew and after ten minutes I'd always want to rush off and write a new play.

One Nottingham playwright Giles mentioned was Nick Wood, who happened to sit next to me that night at The Glee Club, one of the performance venues that has sprung up alongside Nottingham Canal. In my previous Nottingham existence Nottingham Canal had all the attraction of a pierced boil, a stretch of sluggish filthy water overlooked by gloomy satanic buildings, bordered by a shadowy narrow towpath along which few would venture. The odd bike frame or car tyre would protrude from the canal, and the keen-eyed may have spotted a scurrying rat making its way along the tired-looking canal bank.

Urban waterways nationwide had undergone a revolution in the previous two decades. The Quayside in Newcastle, once a grimy and forgotten area of deserted warehouses, and the odd rundown pub of sepulchral interior, now heaved with bars, restaurants, new flats, and the eye-catching Millennium pedestrian bridge.

Likewise Nottingham Canal, with the red-brick British Waterways multi-storey building turned into fashionable flats, and young drinkers sat beneath the brightly coloured parasols at the *al fresco* bars.

The Glee Club was mainly a comedy venue. I liked inventing names for new comedy venues. In Newcastle

146

we had The Hyena, also The Grinning Idiot, but I quite fancied Guff4, Laff or even Chortl. Entrepreneurs are free to steal any of the above titles.

This night the Glee Club was hosting the American country singer Laura Cantrell, who last performed in Nottingham six years previously, but had enough fans to see the 400 seat theatre packed. Cantrell had been one of John Peel's favourites, guaranteeing a large cult following. The show was due to start at 7.30pm but by 8.15pm nothing had happened. This was an acceptable convention in the music business, and the audience chatted and drank beer. Imagine such a delay at a professional football match. The fans would riot. I've known only one rock singer break the convention of coming on late, and maybe it was the football ground location that influenced him. Bruce Springsteen was due to play at 6pm at St James Park, Newcastle. As I walked down the hill towards the ground at ten seconds after six, the distinctive opening riff of *Born in the USA* came wafting through the air. Most of the audience missed the first few numbers. I hear the German electric band Kraftwerk are never a microsecond late in starting.

I was on a freebie with novelist David Belbin, who was reviewing the show for the *Post*. Dave introduced me to the playwright Nick Wood. Nick hailed from Rotherham. My brother's family lived there, and during my Sheffield student days I'd worked the Rotherham 'stop weeks' when the steel furnaces were shut down and students hired in to clean them. Filthy work, but well-paid. Nick had done it too. He now lived in Thackeray's Lane, Woodthorpe, close to the Church of the Good Shepherd, but he was too young to remember Father Mooney.

I told him about my month's return to the city of my birth.

"Never go back," said Nick.

He was right. At least not physically. Writers went back all the time in their minds, which was a legitimate exercise. But physically to retrace your steps, to go looking where your former entity had once existed, was dangerous stuff. Nor did I normally indulge it. Except now. Why exactly?

I had no simple answer. It was not to seek the reassurance of some sepia-tinted memory, nor to disappear into a former life. It was not the desire to reacquaint myself with friends from some seemingly halcyon time. It was not to bury myself away from today. None of these appealed. I felt pretty comfortable with the present-day. The nearest explanation I could get was that the whole exercise was an attempt to understand. Though to understand what?

A small postscript to the day: the long hot weather which had been uninterrupted since my arrival in Nottingham had seen various fires destroy parts of Sherwood Forest. With the forest only one fiftieth its original size, we could well do without such conflagrations.

THIS NOTTINGHAM

An Ashfield Labour candidate came under fire for wearing a t-shirt saying trades unionists would 'Dance on Margaret Thatcher's grave.'

FRIDAY MAY 6

THE TRENT BRIDGE FOOL AND THE DANCE TO THE RITUAL OF LIME

One reason for returning to Sherwood Estate after almost half a century was the intriguing prospect of Mortimer Mark II journeying through the territory of Mortimer Mark I. But day by day the estate was retreating from me. This was a trend that originally troubled me, and one I felt I must resist. I slowly realised such resistance was wrong. I had no rights, no possession of the past. If it did not want me, so be it. Why should it? What did not fit, did not fit. In the next few days I would come to an important decision symbolising how much my expectations had changed.

Meantime, sporting matters loomed large. Tomorrow would be one of the biggest days in Nottingham's football history. If Forest avoided defeat at Crystal Palace, they'd be in the play-offs for the Premiership. If County avoided defeat at home against Division One champions Brighton, they would avoid relegation.

Nottinghamshire's third erstwhile football league team, Mansfield Town, had recently dropped down to the Blue Square Premier League, but in an attempt to recover some past glory were on the same day playing at Wembley to contest the FA Trophy Final. To add to the curiosity, they were playing a team from the North-East, Darlington FC.

Should we wish to make this day even more coincidentally curious, I should mention that on Sunday Whitley Bay FC (the non-league team I supported back in the North-East) were also playing at Wembley, where they appeared in the final of the FA Vase for the third consecutive year. Can you stand another coincidence? Whitley Bay's opponents were also from the East Midlands — Coalville FC.

I'd toyed with the idea of travelling to Wembley for the Whitley Bay game. My son Dylan and I had been the previous two seasons, but I argued that this month belonged to Nottingham, with no skiving off.

Meantime a dilemma had presented itself at 85 Danethorpe Vale. On Sunday, Veronica, Valerie's daughter with her previous partner, was coming over from her Amsterdam home and the three were going out for Sunday lunch. "We're going to Bardills again, and she'd love to meet you," said Valerie.

The dilemma was that my dislike of Bardills was in equal measure to Derrick and Valerie's affection for the place. The Mortimer sense of discretion had prevented me from saying anything, but now the prospect of a return visit filled me with gloom and dismay. Let me get it off my chest. Eating at Bardills felt like eating in a large and noisy works canteen. I found the food luke-warm, bland and overpriced, the beef underdone, the chef's tinny radio off-putting. Basically, I had a Bardills problem, though these considerations apart, I'd had the time of my life.

I now had three options. Firstly, simply to make my excuses and not go. This would work on one level but would mean I'd not meet Veronica. Secondly, go to Bardills and say nothing. This way I got to meet Veronica, but would feel a bit of a sham. Thirdly, come clean about my dislike of Bardills, but go anyway. The third option would leave me feeling less fraudulent, and possibly the truth might free me. I might even enjoy the beef second time around.

The Bardills dilemma crystallised the potential problems of a person plonking himself down on an estate to live four weeks in close contact with two virtual strangers, and all this 48 years and several galaxies removed from his previous life there. For the three of us it meant a rapid readjustment without the luxury of the time required to adapt. We were not eighteen year olds whose clay was still unformed. We had long ploughed our own furrows (watch those metaphors again!). We did

150

things our own way. Age could bring intransigence. Some conflict was inevitable.

So what of Bardills? I needed to mull it over. I wanted to make the visit of Valerie's daughter a success story, unlike the mess I'd made with Derrick's son so far.

That day, there was no better place for such mulling over than Trent Bridge, the world-famous cricket ground of Nottinghamshire CCC, and one of the country's leading Test venues. Cricket had never filled me with the passion of football, yet with the advancing years my football passion diluted as I saw the professional game grow increasingly soured and cynical.

I'd made several recent visits to the one-day internationals at Durham CCC's Riverside Ground in Chester-le-Street, though I'd not been to Trent Bridge for more than half a century. On my previous visit I'd seen the legendary Middlesex batsman Denis Compton (only one 'n' of course — two would have been common). Compton was a star of the England cricket team but also

Trent Bridge — where I could choose any row, in any of the five stands

played professional football for Arsenal, an unthinkable combination these days.

A handsome, charismatic cricketer, a public schoolboy in the Biggles mould, Compton was considered the height of sophistication and glamour. He was contracted to do advertisements for Brylcreem, where he was known by the soubriquet, *The Four Figure Man*. This suggested that the measure of success was someone who earned an annual income of a grand — one thousand pounds, the kind of money a modern footballer would be paid to be filmed swigging from a branded drink when interviewed after the final whistle.

To walk into Trent Bridge that balmy Spring day, to see that wondrous ground spread out before me, to observe the white-flannelled players cracking leather on willow on that luxuriously verdant surface, with maybe a couple of thousand people sprinkled round the four sides of the ground, was to experience a sense of Buddhist calm. If football were Kung Fu, then this was meditation. The occasional ripple of applause was the gentle lap of a wave. And whereas a football match was often a closed cauldron of emotion, a game of county cricket was airy, spacious and as light as a feather.

A day's ticket at Trent Bridge, which would allow you seven hours of viewing, was £8.00 (senior) whereas ninety minutes of football at Forest's City Ground would set you back £24.

I could not only choose any seat in the ground, I could choose any row in any one of the five stands. These stands were of vastly different design, and not liked by everyone, but they worked for me. The Radcliffe Road End, with its five terracotta towers, the central one of which housed the clock, was in distinctive pale brick with a darker brick inlay; it was impressive but not imposing. The newest stand had a roof like a billowing sail. And the ground's floodlights were unlike any I'd seen: giant shower heads or watering cans, at first glance comic, at the next menacing like some towering aliens. Trent Bridge was

152

about modernity, while not forgetting cricket's great traditions.

In the toilets came the luxury of a leisurely and solitary pee, whereas at a football game you queued for several minutes, a slow shuffle to the urinal where you stood in a long line of men cascading forth like Niagara.

This calm sense of civilisation stretched to the politeness of the signs which adverbially requested that you "Kindly Keep off the Grass."

In football you were penned into your restricted area. Here I strode leisurely round the entire ground, able to study the two hi-tec electronic scoreboards. Trent Bridge had boasted one of the world's first electronic scoreboards to replace a generation of unsung men invisibly turning dials, or even earlier, men who hung numbered tiles on hooks. At rural English cricket games there were still men who hung numbered tiles on hooks (and the activity was peculiarly male). Later that summer I would converse with one while watching a game in Bellingham, Northumberland. He even invited me to hang one tile myself, which I did.

My entry into Trent Bridge that day brought a sense of leaving behind a frenetic world of instant gratification to enter an oasis of calm, populated by people for whom life unfurled at a leisurely non-stressful pace. I realised part of this was to do with the ageing process — most of the spectators were around my own age — and realised also that to be exposed to such serenity continually might leave me soporifically inactive, but on this particular day I bathed in its sweet untroubled waters.

The cricket itself was absorbing. Fighting back against a massive Yorkshire first innings total of 534, and already having lost three early wickets, Notts were in a precarious position. But as the spectators knew, the recovery, if there were to be a recovery, would be slow, hard-won and painstaking, an attempt over the course of an entire day for the Notts batsmen slowly to

153

claw their way back into the game. We the spectators were as patient in this desire as were the batsmen.

White was still the colour of county cricket, as it was with test cricket. The one-day limited-overs game had gone in for gaudy coloured team kits. The purpose in any sport of two teams wearing different colours was to distinguish one team from the other. As this was not an issue in cricket (any idiot could identify the batsmen), the policy of coloured kits was shown up as the unashamedly money-making marketing exercise it was. You may as well have put chess players in coloured kits. Someone probably will.

Different colours made cricket more tribal. This suited the marketing departments.

Not that teams were without their own colours in the county game — with Notts it was gold and green — but these were small, subtle trimmings on the basic white. County players did now sport numbers plus their names on their backs, but this was functional rather than razzmatazz — it told me who they were. The dominant colour was white. The players wore white, the umpires wore white, and the stewards dotted round the ground wore long white coats. A sizeable number of spectators had white hair.

In the one-day game, the fall of every wicket was accompanied by blaring triumphalist music, an annoying artificiality unloved by every single spectator I knew. How blissful here to have the fallen batsman walk back to the pavilion to nothing more than the natural sounds of rippling applause.

It struck me that in few other stadium-based sports did you leave the field twice in the day to take meals. Had anyone written about what cricketers ate for lunch and tea? I'd always imagined salad and cold meat for the former, with sandwiches, a pot of tea and possibly a slice of chocolate cake for the latter. Did the teams eat together or apart? And what of the umpires? Did they eat alone? And why were there no female umpires?

My own lunchtime involved a walk to the quiet Pavilion Bar where a long line of signed cricket bats was arrayed above a series of black and white photos of former Notts players, stretching back to splendidly bewhiskered gentlemen of the 19th century. Some figures stood out for me, including Reg Simpson, captain in the 1950s and a leading England batsman. I remembered Simpson entering the record books for once bowling underarm for his country, though I have no idea where or when.

On the honours board were several members of the Gunn family, famous Notts cricketers also involved in the manufacture of the renowned Gunn & Moore cricket bat. Until fairly recently the firm still had its own retail premises in the city.

Only once during this balmy and blissful day, when Notts managed to score more than 400 and hence save themselves from defeat, did anything disrupt the calm.

The luxury of being able to circumnavigate the ground sent me off on a full circuit. When walking in front of the Pavilion Road End, I noticed several of the mature gentlemen seated there were hailing me and waving. I waved back, pleased by this manifestation of civility. They continued to hail and wave and when I looked pitch-wards I saw that the Yorkshire players were now also hailing me. How splendidly civil these cricket games were I concluded, only to realise that I was walking directly behind the bowler's arm and hence affecting the concentration and view of the batsman. The waving and hailing was not borne of civility, but an attempt to get an ignorant idiot to sit down and keep still. My embarrassment was equal to breaking into applause at the end of a classical symphony's first movement, which I also once did. I sat down, and at the end of the over, scurried off to find anonymity in another part of the ground.

One of the Yorkshire players was Ryan Sydebotham, an England bowler who until 2010 had been a mainstay of the Notts side. His return to Trent Bridge was greeted with polite applause, in contrast to a similar situation in

155

football, where bile and abuse would have been hurled at the returning player.

The ground was only a fraction full. A football ground four parts empty was depressing. The place became a hollow and echoey shell. In the more cerebral, more sedate, less claustrophobic world of county cricket, an activity which allowed time and space for personal reflection, sparse attendance was less of an issue, even if for the club accountants it would be a matter of some concern.

There were other obvious differences to football. When the Yorkshire player Ashcroft left the field for a few moments, he came and sat among the crowd. Between deliveries, Shazhad, a boundary fieldsman, chatted away to his mates on the front row.

In one-day cricket, alcohol consumption was enormous and facilitated by a small army of men with swollen beer dispensers attached to their backs, which rendered them almost insectoid. Strangely, this mega-consumption rarely led to the alcohol-fuelled disruption common among football fans. I spotted the occasional tippler here, but the drinking was sedate. Many spectators arrived with picnic hampers to make the occasion akin to watching Shakespeare in the Park.

My final curious cricket observation was as follows: it took a fast bowler more time to bowl an over than it did a slow bowler, which seemed against the laws of velocity.

And so that evening to the theatre! Valerie and Derrick were regular visitors to the Theatre Royal, Nottingham, and we all went to see *Goodnight Mister Tom*, David Wood's adaptation of Michelle Magorian's best-selling novel about a young evacuee in the Second World War. This was a syllabus text, and the place was packed with school children. The play got a glowing review in the *Post*, but none of us was particularly impressed. It seemed uninspired, mechanical and sentimental, a piece of functional workaday theatre. The production did not seem excited by itself, and so neither was I.

What I did enjoy was this cultural expedition with Valerie and Derrick, which seemed like new territory in our relationship. I didn't expect many people to view theatre as part of their lifeblood, as it was with me. But I'd always felt a warmth and affection towards all members of a theatre audience, people taking the time and trouble to gather together in celebration of their fellow humans' story-telling. So experiencing the same with my temporary housemates, even if they hadn't appreciated my lemon chicken, had a special resonance.

We took the bus home. Would Derrick and Valerie like to call in at The Five Ways? No thanks. A part fatalistic, part absurdist pattern had developed round my own Five Ways visits. They had little logic. What was I clutching at? Did I not realise my relationship with the pub was in terminal decline?

Again there were few customers, and again I was wrapped in a sense of alienation. I ordered a bottle of Sol, forgetting to enquire about limes, and it came complete with a slice of lemon wedged in the neck.

At this juncture I again produced my own lime (I had plenty left) and suggested to John that he might cut me a slice. He did so silently. The slice of lemon was wedged too deep in the bottle's neck to remove, so I needed to push the lime in on top. This made for a curious combination, Sol with lime and lemon. Who knows, it may become fashionable? I left the pub at 11.10pm, by which time there were only two other customers on the premises, though a couple of men were sat at an outside table.

One asked, "Did ye ger any lime then?"

"No," I replied, "But luckily I carry my own supplies," and I produced from my bag one of the aforesaid unsliced fruits.

With that The Lime Man made his way back to Danethorpe Vale to watch Jools Holland's *Later* show, and wonder how many more times he would cross The Five Ways threshold. Me, not Jools Holland.

THIS NOTTINGHAM

As part of the University of Nottingham Mayfest, boffins will create thunder and lightning on demand in a thrilling one hour spectacular. People with a hearing condition are not encouraged to attend.

SATURDAY MAY 7

A NUMBER 97 EPIPHANY, FANS OF JOY AND DRINKING IN ADVANCE

The realisation was growing that to revisit your childhood territory physically was far removed from revisiting
it in the mind. If this seemed obvious, so be it. Most
important truths were self-evident in hindsight.

There had been a recent mass media fashion for 'going
back'. Mainly this involved celebs returning to the place of
their upbringing, interviewing schoolmasters, shop-
keepers or ex-friends, and cobbling together a few thoughts
for the camera or microphone as they walked down the
thoroughfares of their youth. Why did such programmes
appear to me as superficial, token and lacking any real
commitment? Because that's what they were.

Not being famous was a definite advantage during my
time in Nottingham, as was the lack of cameras, micro-
phones, or any hint of a production or backup team, all of
which tend to distort that wish they seek to record. Just
little old me here, and if this was a necessary isolation for
the purposes of the book, it could also be a pain in the
butt and see me sliding towards self-pity.

Another simple truth to slowly emerge was that I now
lacked any relationship with Sherwood Estate. It ended
in 1963. I still had some relationship with Nottingham as
a city. Over the years I'd made regular visits to the city
itself; it had changed, I had changed, and we'd been able
to check one another's progress. Not so the Estate. I had
walked out of it and never walked back. For such absence
I was now getting my comeuppance.

Thus far I had crossed only one estate threshold
outside of my 85 Danethorpe Vale home. Nor had I made
much impact around Danethorpe Vale itself. How many
people had come flocking to say hello to the returning

159

prodigal? None. Being an extrovert, I grew unduly concerned at not making an impact. Laughable though it was, if I left no indelible impression, I considered it a failure. My original intention was to call the book *An English Estate*, an idea I had now abandoned. I had been away too long.

On this morning I awoke with a moment of epiphany. Since arriving, one unchanging ambition had been to gain access to 97 Danethorpe Vale. This was for me a *sine qua non* of the book, physically to explore that domestic territory that had been my upbringing, that house which was such a part of my being.

And on this day, Saturday May 7, came the realisation that not only was this not going to happen, but there was no reason, given present circumstances, why it should happen.

What right did I have to barge into that house against the wishes of the present occupant, a man who was born there and had lived there for more than thirty years?

Did my own long-gone occupation of that house give me any claims over it? Did I honestly consider my own time in 97 Danethorpe Vale more important or more relevant than Derrick Junior's time? That was conceited nonsense. I had no claim on that property except memory. It was the past and I had to let it go, just as I had to let Sherwood Estate go. I had paid no dues to that house for forty-eight years.

Once I reached this conclusion, a great weight lifted from me; a burdensome expectation which I simply had taken as read was removed, and I was freed from some erroneous compulsion.

Time changed everything; three simple words — and a massive concept.

As if to confirm this moment of epiphany, I decided to donate the four bottles of Sol to Derrick Junior to drink in his own house. In his own time. In his own company.

When back in Cullercoats, I prided myself on being fairly self-sufficient in cooking, washing clothes and ironing. In this house Valerie did almost all the cooking, she also sorted out my washed clothes and left them in neatly folded piles on my bed. If I was quick enough I could get to change my own sheets, but alacrity was required. My evening meal would be on the table at 6pm sharp, and I had only to sit it in my favourite armchair a few moments before a mug of tea appeared.

Naturally I felt guilty at such indulgences, but I realised how I secretly enjoyed them too. I slowly found my way round Valerie's kitchen, though each day I would pull open the small panel above the cooker, expecting to discover shelving, only to set off a noise akin to an industrial wind tunnel. It was the air extractor, a realisation that took three weeks to sink in.

It had also taken me three weeks to visit Meadow Lane, home of my natural team, Notts County. To support a team such as County was continually to defy logic and common sense, to make light of the general misery and unfulfilment such loyalty brings. One endearing aspect of football partisanship was the huge

Notts County, the view from the pitch

161

optimism it inspired, the belief that sunny times were just round the corner. A County supporter had to scrabble for any small crumb of comfort and here on this day was such a potential crumb.

To avoid defeat against Brighton FC, who had already won the Division One title, would mean County would escape relegation. For many teams this would not be an excuse for paroxysms of ecstasy, but for Notts County supporters it was.

It was a pulsating game, a 1–1 draw, which seemed to suit both sides. A tannoy announcement pleading with County fans to stay off the pitch at the final whistle was ignored, and they swarmed onto the grass, making their way in their hundreds to the stand which housed a large contingent of blue and white bedecked Brighton fans. In the front of this stand, stood an unbroken line of yellow-coated police officers. Rival fans had spent much of the ninety minutes taunting one another, so here were the makings of a small Armageddon.

Except no. As the County fans reached the side of the pitch by the stand, and with only the thin yellow line between them and the Brighton fans, something extraordinary happened.

Each set of supporters began to applaud the other. The Brighton fans took up the chant of the County fans, which was "We're staying up!" and changed it to "You're staying up!" which they recited while pointing at their rivals, an act which among football fans normally suggested aggression and hostility, but in this case was an acknowledgement of the other team's achievement. In turn the County fans raised their hands in the air and applauded the Brighton contingent.

In all my years of supporting football at different levels, knowing its potentially irresistible lure but also its Neanderthal, nihilistic tribal tendencies, I was never so moved by such a spontaneous act from sets of rival supporters; the power of large crowds was made manifest. Such power could be terrifying, but on this occasion, it

162

raised the human spirit, it declaimed optimistically about the human race.

Between these two sets of celebrating supporters who were united, almost uniquely, in common celebration, stood the line of police officers, not quite sure just which stance to take.

The *Nottingham Post* had done a big spread about a planned *Holy Gr-ale Trail* of seven pubs selling real ales and ciders, up the half mile strip of Mansfield Road rising from the Victoria Centre up to Forest Road.

Over the years this had become the city's favourite pub crawl, and the four-day festival, as well as celebrating the varied delights of the drinking holes themselves — all linked by a distinctive individuality and non-corporate identity — offered poetry, live music, and a range of freshly cooked food. There was even a Sausage Festival, sausages supplied — naturally — by J.T. Needham & Sons.

In the interests of research I decided to visit all seven hostelries that evening, indulging in only a half pint in each to reduce the chance of becoming legless.

For some daft reason, whenever ordering a half pint, a rare habit, I felt the need to justify myself, making loud noises about not drinking and driving, or that I was just in for a quickie, or some other excuse for eschewing the true masculinity of a pint.

Fairly soon during my odyssey, with poetry, live music, and sausages nowhere to be seen, it became apparent I'd got the wrong weekend. The Festival was in seven days' time. This was too feeble an excuse not to carry on drinking and researching.

In my previous Nottingham existence, I'd rarely visited the pubs on this stretch of Mansfield Road. The usual behaviour pattern was either to drink at one of the three locals (The Five Ways, The Vale or The Garden City) or head down to the city centre. The years of my own drinking apprenticeship were the dark ages of British brewing, with the onset of Watney's Red Barrel, Worthington 'E', Youngers Tartan and other fizzy

163

monstrosities. This was little to do with demand, or consumer choice, but more the big brewers' realisation that keg beer, unlike cask beer, required little care and attention, both of which cost money. Thus the brewers' stunning con-trick: firstly to reduce the supplies of real ale, then justify cutting these supplies because of falling sales.

In one of the country's most successful grassroots movements, the efforts of the real ale pressure group or, as you might say non-pressure group, CAMRA, had seen the mushrooming nationwide of micro-breweries, now numbering more than 8,000. If the Tory Party wanted to see a real Big Society in action, they should look no further, though as the big six brewers provided the Party with funding, it was unlikely.

And so — Mortimer's exclusive pen-picture advance preview of the *Holy Gr-Ale Festival!*

The Rose of England
This splendidly imposing red-brick building once had a tough reputation. Its unpretentious L-shaped bar had sixteen casks stacked on one wall in preparation for the Festival and facing them an impressive twenty pumps along the bar. Nice fish tank. I settled for Green King Harvest Pale.

The Peacock
A beautiful living piece of Victoriana, main room divided by a long chenille curtain; the many giant flickering candles suggested a séance was due. The only remaining Nottingham pub with back-room bell-pulls to order drinks, it has distinctive acid-etched windows round two sides. Hobgoblin Bitter recommended.

The Golden Fleece
Distinctive green décor, and laid-back atmosphere suggesting an Amsterdam bar but bigger. No TV. Progressive music on tap, steps dividing the bar into

three levels, nice wall graphics, young and individual looking clientèle and bar staff. Eye-catching lamps. I slurped a Tiger Bitter.

The Nag's Head
More brightly lit, big plasma screen, and England flags on the wall. The pub darts were Union Jack pattern. Friendly. I had Marston EPA, plus a shot of Sambuca. "I live on that stuff," said the barmaid. The landlady walked in with a bag of limes for behind the bar. Was she expecting me?

The Lincolnshire Poacher
An impressive row of nine separate cask beers. A retro feel and a series of small rooms that kept surprising me, as did the beer garden. Wooden floor, eighty whiskies, no music or TV, slight heritage feel with old Park Drive adverts and the like. When one customer complained a bitter was slightly off, the management withdrew it immediately. I enjoyed the previously unsampled Derby Double Mash, a ruby beer.

Fade Café/Hard to Find
Highly individual, continental café type feel, with rear glass roof, huge plants and wrought iron balconies. Laid-back music and again the surprise of several separate small drinking areas, Bistros One and Two; an outside area as well. I drank Nottingham Blade (Coppice Side Brewery) served in a beautifully elegant glass. No TV.

The seventh planned venue, near Mansfield Road top was **The Forest**, but a £7.00 cover charge for a live band would have made for an expensive half pint, so I declined.

My mind though was set on completing seven watering holes, and I walked the half mile down Mansfield Road hill baptised by a gentle rain, whose rarity made it a more than usually pleasurable experience. I finished my drinking odyssey in **The Grosvenor**. This was very

165

different: giant screens, piped ersatz music, flashing one-armed bandits, and the 'big shed' feel of many chain pubs, with little sense of individuality. The contrast with the rest of my night was great, and the clientèle looked pretty glum. I drank something anonymous, then walked to the centre of Sherwood. By this time the rain had lost its novelty and I grabbed a late bus home.

THIS NOTTINGHAM

People are encouraged to bring their unmarked seedlings to the next Sherwood Market. They will be able to swap them for other seedlings on a table in Mansfield Road.

SUNDAY MAY 8

EATING A STRING BAG, HELEN
FAREWELL, AND A PLACE APART

The writer's worst enemy, it was said, was the empty white
page. For most writers, this now translates as the blank
screen. For my Nottingham purposes it was still the page; a
fountain pen and hard-backed writing book serving for the
book's first draft. Today the page looked incredibly white
and remarkably empty. Later I would see this sudden lack
of creativity as the Nottingham Ten Day Syndrome. It had
been on day ten — the Thursday of the Royal Wedding —
that I'd last experienced such weariness and sense of ennui.
On that day, I'd lacked all motivation, and spent a lot of it
in bed, a place I normally had to bounce out of on waking.

Now it was Day Twenty, and I was similarly afflicted. I
wanted to be gone from this estate. It wanted me here as
little as I myself wanted to be here. I missed Tyneside,
missed my friends and family with a dull ache, and could
muster no interest in continuing to write the book. I lay in
bed till 9am wallowing in self-pity.

Certain externals should have cheered me up. Notts
County had staved off relegation. Nottingham Forest's 3–0
win at Crystal Palace had secured a play-off position and
Whitley Bay's third successive win at Wembley, 3–1 against
Coalville, had guaranteed them a special place in the record
books. None of this seemed to matter. Plus which my
expected solution to the Sunday Lunch dilemma misfired.
Valerie announced that she had booked a meal for her, her
daughter Veronica, Derrick and me at a local Sherwood
restaurant rather than their much loved Bardills. Derrick
looked glum.

Hindsight showed the decision to be less than satisfac-
tory. Out of kindness I'll omit the restaurant's name,
pausing merely to reflect that its pleasant décor and good
reputation were belied by the roast beef which was the

nearest I have come to eating a string bag. When I made some mild complaint to the waitress about its toughness, I was told, "Well, I'm afraid I'm not the chef."

After one particular chewathon, I swallowed the meat, only to find the swallowed portion down my throat was still attached to the unswallowed portion in my mouth, the two portions connected via a kind of umbilical chord. This was not appreciated by my throat muscles and I suffered a series of convulsive retchings — much to the curiosity of other nearby diners. Luckily there was no projectile vomit. I pushed the plate away whereupon Derrick picked up my remaining beef and wrapped it in tinfoil for the foxes. I hope they didn't choke.

The restaurant was named after a 19th century French poet, a fact which brought a piece of spontaneous wit from Veronica who said, "I think it must have been his cow." The poor meat quality reinforced Derrick's firm belief that we should all have gone to Bardills. He may have been right. After sitting mainly in silence during the meal, he rose fifteen minutes before us three and announced he would wait at the car, whereupon Veronica scolded him for sulking.

Veronica was bright-eyed and breezy, with the kind of open optimism inherited from her mum, and a natural humour that was doubly welcome on this day when tensions were in the air, a day when I myself felt slightly less than a million dollars. Her father, Valerie's former husband, died of cancer when she was young. He was Jamaican, and she was one of two daughters, the other, Sylvia, living in London.

Later I cycled up the length of Danethorpe Vale for my final call at Helen's house. My lethargy was such that I dismounted two-thirds of the way up, and pushed. Again Helen opened the door a few inches, and I had the impression of a frightened bird.

"Hello Helen," I said. "I just wondered if the non-slip mat worked OK in the bath."

"Oh," she said, her eyes darting this way and that as if

168

predators lurked, "I haven't had time to try it yet."

I suddenly had the impression of an elderly lady who had been warned, probably by her brother, to have nothing to do with that fellow calling at the door, who may well be a conman and scoundrel intent on robbing the place. If anything, the door was now less open than ever. "Oh well," I said, "I hope you manage to get it sorted out eventually," and I took my leave knowing that I would never set eyes on Helen again, but knowing there was no more to be done.

There were probably millions of Helens round the country, a thought that hardly lightened my less than festive mood.

A call from Ross Bradshaw asked had I considered putting a letter in the *Post* asking for anyone who had been around the estate during my early years to get in touch.

This was a perfectly reasonable and logical enquiry from a publisher, in such circumstances, yet I was as likely to consider it as to dance naked in the Market Square. Slowly the book was moving away from historical documentation and becoming — well, a strange cocktail. Knocking on doorsteps, notebook in hand, simply wasn't it any more. Research, for want of a better word, now consisted of following whatever instinct made its presence felt as I exposed myself to Nottingham 2011. As Peter Sellers might have put it, just '*Being There*'.

On this particular day, all instinct was moribund, dead in the water. It was a day dedicated to inertia. I sat in the armchair watching Topol in *Fiddler on the Roof,* trying to allay a feeling of guilt that I had interfered with the well-established and much loved Sunday routine of lunch at Bardills. Derrick was more withdrawn than normal, and the atmosphere in the house, especially after Veronica's departure, only reinforced the sense of misplacement. Which I couldn't afford. 85 Danethorpe Vale was my safe haven on Sherwood Estate, my bolt-hole, my only sense of home. When I knocked at the front door, they let me in. And on this day, they let in other people too. Not just Veronica, but also a neighbour, Leon, who called mid-evening.

169

Leon's visit emphasised how social habits had changed. A few decades ago, it would be unlikely the TV would be on when someone called, and if so, out of politeness it would be switched off. Now many households would as soon switch off the telly as disconnect the gas supply, and the most that could be hoped for was a turning down of the volume. Think of the TV as a reassuring presence in the corner, flickering away rather as in previous times the open fire would flicker in the grate. How many people would throw a bowl of cold water over the fire when visitors arrived?

Leon was a cheerful, approachable man curious about my Nottingham book, and when sketching in the main details I adopted an enthusiastic persona totally at odds with my current state of mind. He asked was it a memoir, an auto-biography, a diary, or a social document, and I told him to take his pick.

In all the 'out there' books I had written, be it a 500 mile penniless walk through Britain, six months working as a fisherman in the North Sea, travelling through moun-tainous Yemen, spending a winter on Holy Island, or living two months in a Palestinian Refugee Camp, Sherwood Estate was the only territory with which I was previously familiar, though I had paid brief visits to Holy Island. Yet nowhere seemed more alien and impenetrable. In the poverty, squalor and culture shock of Shatila Refugee Camp I had been constantly invited, often with fervent passion, to enter the humble homes and share food. In the small island insularity of Holy Island I became familiar with many homes. Yemeni people opened all doors for me. I found refuge and shelter with total strangers when a penniless traveller. On small fishing boats you were, like it or not, a temporary close-knit community.

Yet Sherwood Estate, 2011, remained mainly a closed book to me, my one-time intimacy and familiarity with the place being the barrier that now separated me from it. To knock on doors here now seemed an artificiality, an unnat-ural force-feeding of the book. Things were both simpler and more complicated than that.

In all those other books I had carried no baggage; I could move freely. Here I was weighed down with so many metaphorical suitcases, I could barely walk.

And then I realised Sherwood Estate had been my trap; it had been the place from which I had needed to escape. In every person's life there was somewhere from which he or she must escape. It was, if you like, a necessary crisis on the road to fulfilment. Sorry, that sounded a bit like one of those self-help books.

My mother had escaped from rural Ireland to make a new life in Nottingham. My father had escaped this estate to recreate himself as a *petit-bourgeois* in posher Redhill. My brother Alex had escaped, first to university then to a life in industry and commerce. I had escaped first the estate, then Nottingham, to redefine myself as a writer. All these escapes were essential, though of variable success.

And what was now a major driving force in my life, books, theatre, the arts, seemed marginal at best for many people on this estate. Partly this was due to the tendency of all us artists, being inevitably immersed in the seductive power of our own creative worlds, to give that same world (of little significance to most) an inflated importance.

Having been on that road to Damascus, I strongly believed that art had the potential to transform lives and to free the mind. But what if I was wrong? What if for a majority of people it was simply peripheral and would remain so, territory neither charted nor likely to be so?

It was this kind of uncomfortable possibility that the estate made me confront. And I was removed from my comfort zone in a different way than being up a Yemeni mountain, out on a small fishing boat in a stormy sea, or living in a small cramped room on a refugee camp. What had once been the familiar had become the alien. But then what else did I expect? Had I not deliberately cast it off?

Or had I always been a stranger on Sherwood Estate, something merely confirmed by the passage of almost half a century, and my eventual return?

Sunday — hence no *Post* titbit.

171

MONDAY MAY 9

FROM BIRO TO LIDO
AND BITTER SWEET HOME

I awoke, and for no logical reason into my mind came a vision of the plaque outside The Peacock, the second pub on my recent seven-venue Mansfield Road odyssey. The plaque recorded The Peacock as the occasional watering hole of Nottingham's most renowned literary son, D.H. Lawrence.

The message was clear; the book's current was directing me to Lawrence's birthplace, in the small mining town of Eastwood on the Notts/Derbys border. I had played football in Eastwood during my Nottingham years, but made no literary pilgrimage to the birthplace, and only one brief visit since.

I resolved to go the following day. It was a journey of eight or nine miles and I would travel by bike, giving an extra sense of adventure. I had no idea what I was looking for, only that I needed to go.

The decision cheered me, and on my cycle ride up Danethorpe Vale that morning, I managed the full gradient without dismounting, puffing in triumph at the summit.

One of my regular ports of call on Mansfield Road, Sherwood, was the *mm...deli* on the corner of Wilkinson Street, run for the last ten years by southerner Janet Heineman. It was down to Janet that the giant mural on the same corner had been created. The artist was James Grant. This was the second mural, the first, a version of *The Creation* by Leonardo da Vinci, had been vandalised by a paint thrower, so in its place we had a lively and colourful Sherwood collage, part of the area's small but impressive display of psychedelia, not quite Haight-Ashbury of the Sixties but enough to suggest some kind of alternative beating heart.

172

The top of the long Danethorpe Vale gradient — a regular battle on my bike

The deli itself did its bit, being a good place to chill out, with home-made soup at £2.00 and various periodicals spread around that you'd be unlikely to find in WH Smith. I came across for the first time a magazine called *The Left Lion*, part of Nottingham's counter-culture. The title refers to the famous stone lions in front of The Council House in Slab Square.

More Sherwood psychedelia

There was a mention in *The Left Lion* of Lord Biro, one of Nottingham's more eccentric poets. To be a small press poetry publisher (as I had been since 1973) was to know of the existence of Lord Biro, for at one time or another every such publisher was trained in his Lordship's sights. I had never published any of his work, though I had seen his poems in various publications, and knew his reputation as an oddball, a curio, a non-establishment figure. I loved the name with its echoes both of Nottingham's associations with Lord Byron, and the humble low-tech writing implement, and imagined him as a wild Byronic figure, a dishevelled agitator. I arranged to meet up with him that evening in a Carrington pub. Carrington was the district south of Sherwood, an area little-known to me during my Nottingham years, somewhere we simply passed through with barely a second glance *en route* to our city centre shenanigans.

We young turks would visit only one place in Carrington: the Lido, an outdoor swimming pool which was among a series of Nottingham lidos popular in the 50s and early 60s, all of which had long since closed. Global warming could be the excuse to reopen them. The main memory of Carrington Lido was being thrown off the top diving board by the one-time Notts County centre-half, Pete Russell. Russell, with the physique of Buzz Lightyear, would hurl us young lads, squealing part from delight, part from terror, into the water below. It was something of a status symbol to have been thrown off the top board by Pete Russell, and there was always a queue.

Carrington Lido was now a Pirate's Play area for children, and behind it was the pub, The Gladstone, tucked away on Loscoe Road only yards from the busy Mansfield Road.

According to Ross Bradshaw, who was already *in situ* when I walked in, The Gladstone was the hub of the area's alternative society. I grew up, as all young men, with the belief I was different, though my youth was never very alternative, with barely a radical idea in my head before the age of twenty-one. The Gladstone would not have interested me.

As you'd expect, the pub was not owned by Hungry Horse, Beefeater, Tuck In, The Garrulous Guzzler or any other chain. There was no TV, two traditional bars, with a selection of cask beers lining the public bar. This bar contained its own ad-hoc library stretching the length of

175

one wall. The clientèle, of mixed age, looked a thoughtful bunch and were engaged in conversation in the same manner I imagined pertained in London's 18th century coffee houses. Next to the pub was Carrington Pottery, plus a local silversmith. The large elegant houses in the area were now mainly in multi-occupation, and there was a pleasant small park which I circumnavigated twice — such perambulating arboreal delights always able to lift the spirits.

Lord Biro (*aka* Dave Bishop) was more avuncular and middle-aged than in my imagination, and also quite amiable for an iconoclast. He stood in the local election for the Militant Elvis Anti-Tesco Popular Front party, and gained 322 votes. He had made his own contribution to the Royal Wedding, namely satirical drawings of various Royals, including The Queen, Kate, William and Princess Beatrice. These he had turned into souvenir t-shirts.

The t-shirts were on display (and also on sale at £10 apiece) in the store Aikon Leisure in the slightly rundown and eccentric West End Arcade in the city centre.

Ross Bradshaw mentioned a particular Lord Biro poem he liked, and as befitted a genuine eccentric, his Lordship couldn't remember having written it. It was only four words long, and is a genuine piece of Nottingham culture, though may make little sense to outsiders. Here it is:

PUB
Shippo's, mild.
Home,
Bitter.

Cultural and regional references are as follows. Two of the main Nottingham breweries, as readers of this book should know, were Shipstone's (Shippo's) and Home Breweries, both gobbled up by large corporates and now closed down. In the East Midlands, mild beer as well as bitter was still a popular drink. Local CAMRA activists

176

had recently launched *A Walk on the Mild Side* for perambulating quaffers, so this short punny poem could be the anthem of a Nottingham man finding the peace of his local more attractive than the acrimony of domestic life, and it packs quite a bit into its few words.

The prospect of my Eastwood trip the next day had slightly lifted the spirits, as had a few pints in The Gladstone, though I felt a returning listlessness, an atypical sense of *ennui* as I headed back towards the estate, which for me was now a negative force.

THIS NOTTINGHAM

A Dutch couple are such fans of Robin Hood that they have come to St Mary's Church in Edwinstowe to marry — it's reputed to be where Robin and Maid Marian said, "I do."

Aike Bosman and Annika Van Beers tied the knot yesterday.

TUESDAY MAY 10

THE IRRESISTIBLE LURE OF EASTWOOD, JAM SPONGE AND LAWRENCE'S FORGOTTEN NAME

As soon as I jumped in the saddle and set off on the ride to Eastwood, the two-wheel therapy began to kick in. There was a feeling of adventure, that 'in touch' sense known to all cyclists, and denied to all motorists. To cycle was to be released. There was also a sense of homage, a journey by this 'umble returning native to pay homage to a major Nottingham writer.

Eastwood was — well, westward from Sherwood, the first half of the journey pleasantly flat as I cycled along the city ring roads, Valley Road, leading onto Western Boulevard, then out through Nuthall, Cinderhill and into Kimberley,

I passed a pub in Kimberley, The Three Ponds, which evoked a partially buried memory of a one-time girlfriend who lived nearby. She was a nurse, and during our relationship she spent a training spell in Sheffield, coming back to Nottingham each weekend. On Sunday evenings, usually after a drink in The Three Ponds, I'd sit with her in the back seat of her father's car as he drove the 35 miles to Sheffield, and we two would indulge in secret, erotic fumblings while still facing forward and carrying on a perfectly sensible and grown-up conversation with her dad.

The memory came back and took me unawares, washed over me with a great and heavy sadness, the realisation that such illicit moments were gone forever. As we get older, the official line is that we find comfort in the past. Old people's homes are full of semi-comatose folk encouraged to reminisce or sing *The White Cliffs of Dover*. Yet much of the past was painful, melancholic. In this regard, writers are lucky. They can shape the past to their purposes.

Under the M1 and through Kimberley, you could taste Lawrence on your lips with the appearance of such places as the forbidding out-of-time red-brick exterior of Kimberley Miners' Welfare, or the equally forbidding-looking 1893 Greasley Board School. Lawrence himself went to a board school.

Yet this was 2011. And down the bottom of the hill, before turning up towards Eastwood (the terrain now having got much hillier) was the shining new Giltbrook Retail Park, with its huge windowless outlets such as IKEA, and the Family Entertainment Centre, *Escape*.

I'd never read Lawrence when living in Nottingham, nor that many other authors either. I'd like to say I was the shy, sensitive boy in the corner protected by a book against the bellowing loudmouth bullies, but it's not true. I often bellowed myself. Reading and talking about novels was not part of the Sherwood Estate mixture. For French and German A-levels, I read the likes of Maupassant, Molière, Goethe and 19th century French poets such as Baudelaire and Gautier, and Victor Hugo. These made a big impression on me, a fact I failed to realise at the time. They were merely a part of school, which meant they were something in principle I was against, even as deep inside, I was absorbing them, storing them like a savings account.

There had been few books at 97 Danethorpe Vale; my mates read little, and I held not a single visual memory of either my mother or father sitting reading a book. What reading I did was in isolation. Only when away from Nottingham did reading become a normal and essential part of life.

When I did get to read Lawrence's work, it had a big effect on me, as if he understood life on a level whose exis-tence I hadn't previously known. Nor was this just 'intellectual' stuff, but physical too, the passions that drove and often destroyed men and women. I read *Sons*

179

and Lovers, Women in Love and *The Rainbow* in fairly quick succession — dark intense novels, sometimes over-preachy, but giving a whole new perspective to both my own life and where I'd grown up. I read some of his poems, and later saw some of his plays.

Once he left Eastwood, Lawrence barely returned, roaming Europe and North America, though he still called his place of birth "the country of my heart". The great descriptive power he brought to bear on his native surroundings ironically only realised its full potential once he was free of them.

Onwards towards Eastwood. I passed two contrasting hostelries: on one corner a distinctive curved pub called *The Greasley Castle*, and a few yards distant the strangely named *The Man in Space*, whose title and horrendous Sixties matchbox architecture suggested it was built in 1969 to celebrate Neil Armstrong's first moon walk. It was now boarded up and had fallen out of orbit.

Eastwood was not the kind of town to stick up large signs announcing *You Are Now in D.H. Lawrence Country!* or the kind to make a major industry of its world-famous author, who died in 1930.

Historically Eastwood always had an ambivalent atti-tude towards its literary son, which was more refreshing than sticking him on a pedestal, figuratively or in reality. You could, with a little effort, get hold of The Blue Line Trail (25p), an informative coloured leaflet leading you around twenty Eastwood locations important in the author's life and/or mentioned in his novels, including two pubs, two churches, two schools, four houses and two farms. Curiously, the smallest type on the brochure's front cover was reserved for the writer's name.

Riding my bike through Eastwood, which retained a close-knit working-class feel, a town where people still regularly hailed one another across the street, I spotted few outward Lawrentian references. There was The Lawrence Veterinary Centre, which receptionist Donna Mace told me had changed its name from the John Mason

180

Centre in the 90s, but the only other commercial example spotted was a high street outlet called Lawrencetown Jewellery. I missed the Lawrence Snackery though.

Eastwood, like many mining towns, was not particularly attractive; there were new buildings, but the tightly packed terraces of Lawrence's time were still much in evidence. If the town itself could seem cramped, its often steep streets offered contrasting glimpses of the beautiful rolling countryside in which it was set.

The author's birthplace, a small mining cottage at 8a Victoria Street, was now a Lawrence museum, two-up, two down, with one attic room.

I arrived at the museum ten minutes late for the 1.45pm guided tour. As no-one else had turned up, the guide Kath Hall took me on it anyway. We entered the small darkish rooms with their cast-iron beds, their small open fires, their washbowls and jugs, their narrow windows; we clambered to the attic up a narrow staircase steep enough to scrape your nose on the step above as

The Lawrence museum

Kath spoke with an infectious enthusiasm about Lawrence and his life. He was born on September 11, 1885 (9/11 if you will) and Victoria Street was the first of four Eastwood residencies as the family slowly moved up the social scale. Their final Eastwood home, in Lynncroft, was semi-detached, with an inside toilet.

His father Arthur was a miner, his mother Lydia, from Ancroft in Manchester, was slightly higher up the social scale, and, Kath told me, some say that when the two met, Lydia misunderstood the nature of his work, which he described as 'a mining contractor'. She was left in no doubt the first day he arrived home from the pit, so blackened she failed to recognise him.

It was mainly Lydia's ambition, once she realised the squalor and the drudgery she had let herself in for, that saw the family slowly improve their lot. Kath took me into the front parlour, whose window also served as a shop display of knitted garments which Lydia would sell for extra pin money. Any customers would walk round to the back door for service.

"The front parlour was rarely used, except for special occasions, nor the front door, " said Kath. This habit had passed on. At 85 Danethorpe Vale the front room was used for storage. During my childhood at 97 we rarely ventured into the front room, again except for special occasions. And the front door was never used. When we'd finished this personalised tour, Kath left me to mooch around the small souvenir shop. There was no-one waiting for the next timetabled tour either.

Opposite the house/museum was The White Peacock café. *The White Peacock* was Lawrence's first novel. This was not some twee tearoom with the doilies and cake stands you might expect at a Jane Austen pilgrimage site, but an unpretentious and functional café, with faded place mats and half a dozen customers with broad local accents, including two bulky lasses in trackies. They were tucking into generous meat-and-two-veg dinners. I ate a hearty meal, leaving enough room for a splendid jam sponge and custard. Hungry work, this cycling.

Thinking of my return to Sherwood Estate, I wondered what Lawrence would have made of returning to live for a month in Victoria Street, Eastwood. He left his home town at the age of 23, two years later than me. I realised that for Lawrence, such a return would have been inconceivable. He wrote about his native city constantly, with no need to go back. I wrote about it rarely. And hence returned.

By my age Lawrence was long dead, but I found myself making comparisons. We both had three 'first' names — he liked to forget this third, William, calling himself just D.H. for David Herbert. Mine are Peter John Granville, should you be interested. Lawrence's first job in Nottingham was for a false-limb manufacturer. Mine was for a false-teeth merchant. His final address in Eastwood was 97 Lynnthorpe. My final address in Sherwood was 97 Danethorpe Vale. And both the Mortimer and Lawrence families struggled to break free of their social conditions and standing.

All this combined inside me to strange effect. I had now accepted I would not gain access to 97 Danethorpe Vale, Sherwood. Thus, visiting 8a Victoria Street, Eastwood, the house of Lawrence's upbringing, became a kind of surrogate, an unlikely link to my own one-time Nottingham abode. He was a literary giant from almost a century past, I was a humble scribbler. Yet I knew, as I sat in The White Peacock café, and stared across the narrow steep road to his birthplace, what had drawn me here, and felt at that moment extraordinarily close to the Nottingham spirit of D.H. Lawrence, as if he had invited me here specifically to spend time in 8a Victoria Street.

Fascinating though the other Lawrence Blue Trail locations doubtless were, I was not moved to visit them. Home was where the heart was.

Next to the birthplace was Scargill Walk, and passing through Kimberley I'd noticed Scargill Avenue. Despite

183

the area's strong mining traditions, neither of these were connected with King Arthur of the 1984–85 miners' strike fame, whose aftermath, the death of the industry, had knocked much of the stuffing out of Eastwood as it had many mining towns.

Lawrence died in a French sanatorium in 1930, though his niece Joan was still alive at the age of 90 at the time of this book's publication.

On the long cycle home, I took a small diversion through Old Basford to check out the magnificent red-brick building that was once Shipstone's Brewery. The brewery had gone but the splendid edifice was still used commercially by numerous smaller outfits. The main tower had a Stalinesque grandeur, and the brewery's distinctive trademark was still in place, though this one-time red star was now simply a star — no red.

This chapter devoted mainly to D.H. Lawrence seems a good place to look at some contemporary Nottingham novelists I came to read or reread via my month-long odyssey to my native city.

Two other celebrated Nottingham writers stayed put for longer than Lawrence. Stanley Middleton grew up in Bulwell, and moved only a few miles to Sherwood during his entire life. He attended High Pavement Grammar School, then Nottingham University, then returned to High Pavement to teach for his whole career. One of his pupils was me. A spell of National Service in India was Middleton's only significant time absent from the city, Nottingham was central to all his books, though he called the city Beechnall. Stanley Middleton wrote 45 novels, one of which *Holiday*, won the Booker Prize.

John Harvey, who bases his Charlie Resnick detective novels in the city, was born in London, taught in Nottingham in the 60s, then returned to do an MA at Nottingham University. He stayed in the city a further fourteen years — the moral being that there is no moral, except every writer has to make their own choice. Live in the Peruvian mountains, or the house you grew up in, or

184

just stick around a while — whichever allows you to write.

I'd never been a great reader of detective novels, or crime fiction as it is now called, usually content to wait for the film or TV versions which I could digest in an hour or so. Recent years have seen vociferous claims for the genre to be considered serious literature. So it was time to read a John Harvey novel. General advice was that *Lonely Hearts* was among his best — the book is not to be confused with Nathanael West's novel *Miss Lonelyhearts,* set in New York of 1933.

Harvey is a prolific writer and his detective, Charlie Resnick, is known to millions of TV viewers. Few writers in this field have also worked in small press publishing, but Harvey has, with *Slow Dancer Press.* Like Stanley Middleton, he doesn't mention the word Nottingham, referring to it as 'the city', but the many locations, streets, districts and pubs mentioned by name leave the reader in no doubt.

Resnick is overweight, with stains on his tie; he supports the less fashionable Nottingham football team, Notts County, loves jazz and names his four cats, which sleep on his bed, after jazz musicians.

He's part of a police team often racist, cynical, and always watching their backs. *Lonely Hearts* is a book whose plot – two women are brutally raped and murdered — is sucked into the twilight world of newspaper personal ads, and is set before computer dating really took off. Technology now moves so fast, references to such things as floppy discs almost make this an historical novel.

The circumstances are often downbeat, the characters often unpleasant, yet I can sense Harvey's love of the city and its edge, and quite rightly his work is now seen as an important part of contemporary Nottingham culture. He also writes well, not an attribute of all crime literature authors. Try this observation: 'Sheppard's hand was damp and cloying. And Resnick was reminded of squeezing the water from spinach, cooked and rinsed.'

185

During the course of the book Resnick embarks on an affair with a married social worker, but a romantic novel it ain't. You don't much like any of the characters, but you still want to read about them.

All of which couldn't quite convince me to rush into reading great swathes of the detective genre; maybe it's the fact that whatever the literary claims made by the protagonists, in the books you can nearly always hear the machinery moving.

But, Lawrence, Harvey and Middleton all bring to their native city an authenticity, a sense of geographical reality less evident in towns or cities that have not inspired such works. We, the natives, are flattered that these writers chose to root their literary creations in the same city where our own clay was formed.

Not that all Nottingham novelists display their birth-place credentials. I'm aware the above are all male, so mentioning Julie Myerson is both a slight redress of the gender imbalance, and also an example of a Nottingham novelist for whom a sense of place is not a priority. Myerson is a regular on the BBC2 arts programme *Late Night Review*, where her mixture of brains and good looks combine to telling effect. Yet possibly only Nottingham-ians reading her début novel, *Sleepwalking*, would spot the occasional small reference to the city locations.

Neither Nottingham nor London — where most of the novel takes place — is evoked to any degree, the author being more interested in character than location, and I doubt many Myerson readers identify her with a partic-ular town.

The novel concerns a married woman who embarks on an affair when eight months pregnant, while at the same time regularly seeing the ghost of a young boy. An unhappy marriage seems almost a given for a modern domestic novel (where is the great novel about a happy marriage?) but Myerson is her own woman for all that, and I can think of no other novel where a wife 'strays' so late in a pregnancy. The book displays a physicality and

186

passion not the hallmark of Middleton or Harvey, but of which Lawrence would have approved, and it also has a dark father figure with some similarities to Morrel in *Sons and Lovers*. Which is more or less the end of the Nottingham links.

In the North East I came to know another writer whose school days were spent in Nottingham. Michael Standen, who died in 2008, moved with his wife Valerie up to Durham City, where I met them. I had no idea of the Nottingham connection till I spotted him wearing a tie familiar to me which I hadn't seen for a quarter of a century — that of High Pavement Grammar School. Michael Standen was also a former pupil, though earlier than me, and was also taught by Stanley Middleton. At his suggestion, the two of us travelled down some years ago to Nottingham for High Pavement School's 200th anniversary celebrations. I say at his suggestion, as revisiting the school for any purpose was a thought never previously entering my head.

In Durham, Michael helped run the Colpitts Poetry Reading Centre and edit *Other Poetry* magazine. He was a wise and gentle man whose company you always eagerly anticipated, and his first novel, *Start Somewhere* published by Heinemann in 1965, was received with great enthusiasm. *The Guardian* called it 'highly accomplished' and for *The Observer* it was 'rich in the home-distilled aphorisms and idealistic resolutions of the young.' The book was recently republished by the Nottingham-based Shoestring Press, and I read it for the first time, realising, to my shame, just how few contemporary Nottingham novels I'd read prior to my writing this book. It was a place I'd left behind in more ways than one.

Start Somewhere is full of quality writing, and located in a Nottingham it has no problems naming; curiously an early and the most relevant incident in the novel tales place in the Arboretum area (see Mortimer's first job, and see Graham Greene's short tenure in the city).

The story centres on the growing pains of a group of older pupils in a Nottingham school, and the dialogue has a similar muscular intellect to Stanley Middleton's, who I suspect was a big influence. Though most of the characters are young, the book in no way is aimed at the *yoof* market. I'm not sure it's aimed at any particular market, except those who appreciate intelligent writing, which is as it should be. Yet the pupils' sense of maturity, though troubled, meant they hailed from a different planet to myself and my Sherwood contemporaries.

Standen brought out another three novels with Heinemann. He wrote more, but the company didn't publish them, and his writing career went into relative obscurity as his early work went out of print. While in Durham, the situation was partly redeemed with the North-East based Flambard Press bringing out his poems and short stories. But no more novels.

While in the Nottingham novels department, a word for Jenny McLeod's book, *Stuck up a Tree*. She's the only black Nottingham novelist I've featured, and her book, though domestic, and again with a backdrop of a wobbly relationship, achieves, via its Jamaican/UK mix, an exotica not evident in the others.

I also warmed to it because of its interest (obsession?) with food — the West Indian variety, not bangers and mash. Throughout characters are cooking, eating, or talking about the likes of fried plantains, goatfish, roast breadfruit, sweet dumplings, red peas with coconut milk and scallion, *al dente* cho-chos, along with quantities of dark rum, and when food is not actually being indulged, it serves as a metaphor in the novel. The plot concerns the well-to-do London caterer Ella returning north to her family roots for her mother's funeral — a woman who curiously drowned in a bowl of fritter mixture (more food) after suffering a heart attack. Since moving south Ella's taken up with a white boyfriend, and her lifestyle is vastly different to that of her large family, who she plans to visit and then depart from as quickly as possible.

Unlike the other Nottingham novels featured in this book, Jenny McLeod's is dominated by women, sometimes there is an entire chapter without a single male. The male characters who do feature tend to be more passive, less interesting.

And the direct speech is written in a sing-song West Indian patois so infectious that the moment we read it, we hear it as if spoken out loud.

"Him was such a gentleman, him bring a whole bag a yam come throw down in front a Puppa."

Ella's planned sharp exit from her home doesn't quite work out. With a Stephen King touch, she finds every attempt to leave eventually brings her back to the Pink House (literally — every inch of it painted pink) of her upbringing. Just as I couldn't gain access to the house of my own childhood, Ella cannot escape hers. As she struggles to distance herself from her past Ella comes to realise that, 'she was one of them. No matter how many times she tried to take off the suit of clothes she thought were uncomfortable, they grew back and she had to remember she was one of them.' And it's here, in this house, that a terrible secret is eventually revealed. This is a book about families and where we belong, and so is mine in a way, so that's alright.

Except Hanville, the invented name of the town Ella returns to from London, bears not the slightest resemblance to Nottingham. The only hint of the real location comes in the sentence, 'The church with its crooked spire stuck out, the highest building in town,' which could mean we were talking about nearby Chesterfield, not a town overburdened by the attentions of novelists.

I'd left Nottingham before I first read Alan Sillitoe's definitive novel *Saturday Night and Sunday Morning*, though I caught the Karel Reisz film — screenplay by Sillitoe himself — on its 1960 release while still living on Sherwood Estate. Albert Finney played the young anti-hero Arthur Seaton and I'd never seen or heard anyone like him in film. I felt the same reading the novel a few years later, and rereading it, I realised how it plugs me directly into the Nottingham of my adolescence; a fact which both excites and disturbs me.

Delving into contemporary Nottingham novels has been an education. Other Nottingham novels had an impact, but *Saturday Night* blew me away, and not only for the fact it mentions Notts County in the second paragraph. It is a truly subversive book: Seaton is an accomplished liar, a heavy drinker, he's involved in fights; he sleeps with his best friend's wife, and then her sister (who herself is married), he cheats his friends at poker; at one stage he and his mate help a drunk to his front door, but not before first checking his wallet for cash. He has no respect for authority, government, rules, employers or institutions, and believes life is one long battle against 'them' trapping you. Arthur Seaton has removed himself from our normal responsibilities, and if there is an inevitability that life will eventually tame him, we know he will go down fighting.

"Everyone in the world was caught somehow, one way or another, and those that weren't, were always on the way to it," he says. Finally he himself is 'caught', engaged to be married to Doreen after his adventures with different married women see him badly beaten up. Yet in the final pages, as he fishes by the canal bank, while still raging against the world, he acknowledges his immediate fate with a certain stoicism and a rare example of self-awareness. No-one escapes forever.

Sillitoe's sparse style vividly conjures a Nottingham of trolley buses, sluggish canals, rowdy pubs, teddy boys, factory floors, Saturday-night suits, sprawling, chaotic families, and the annual Goose Fair. Though he was writing of a time a few years prior to my own adolescence, I tasted the city of my youth on every page.

Seaton is a nihilistic hedonist, and in many ways a thoroughly unlikeable character. Yet there is, at least for me, an uncomfortable charisma about him, a barely admissible, indefensible yearning for such casting off of

190

responsibility, something to do with that Bob Dylan quote that only the honest can truly live outside the law. The book has none of the condescension to the working classes utilised by many writers. Sillitoe is totally unsentimental, non-judgemental, and never seeks easy sympathy for his main character. His closely detailed descriptions of Seaton's working day on the Raleigh bike factory floor reminded me that, unlike most writers, Sillitoe served his time in such places.

Seaton thinks on his feet, has a spirited if muddled energy, a sardonic humour; he believes that somehow he will triumph against 'the bastards' (more or less everyone else). For this reason, part of us wants to be part of him. When I first came across the character, all of me wanted to be all of him. He was toxic — and intoxicating. I had found a voice for my own unreconstructed life. Take his justification for sleeping with married women, a strange mixture of delusion, exploitation and female support. Sillitoe writes:

'He had no pity for a 'slow' husband. There was something lacking in them... something that they, the 'slow' husbands could easily rectify if they became less selfish, brightened up their ideas and looked after their wives a bit better.'

I knew that feeling. I'd been there.

The book is personal but also political; most politicians prefer to not to consider the uncomfortable reality of the Arthur Seatons of this world. The writing is occasionally harrowing — try the description of a back-street abortion — and the imagery also illustrates Sillitoe's poetic gifts, such as the night-time double-decker bus 'like a lighted greenhouse, growing people.'

Saturday Night and Sunday Morning was published in 1958, after several rejections from publishers, and that year won *The Observer* Best Novel of the Year Award, and the Authors' Club prize for Best First Novel.

No other novel captured the muddled, tortuous, cruel, occasionally exhilarating sense of that generation —

191

more or less my generation — growing up as working class lads in Nottingham, a city which granted Alan Sillitoe its Freedom in 2008.

And to write it, the author had to be far distant from the place.

Forty years later he wrote the sequel *Birthday*, with Arthur Seaton now in his sixties. I could not bear the prospect of reading it.

I have a small comic and bloody anecdote about Allan Sillitoe. It was 1973, and Sillitoe was reading at Newcastle's famous poetry centre, Morden Tower. The poet Tom Pickard and his wife Connie, who ran the Tower, put Sillitoe up at their bohemian Gateshead flat where I lived at the time. Connie made a meal of home-made beefburgers. I tasted mine and it was only half-cooked.

"How's your beefburger, Pete?" asked Connie. I was slightly in awe of the company and not wanting to cause a fuss. "Fine, fine" I answered.

"Mine's not cooked," said Sillitoe and pushed away his plate.

"Ours as well," said Tom and Connie, and did likewise. I was left to eat my awful bloody concoction alone. Arthur Seaton would have chucked the thing out the window.

THIS NOTTINGHAM

Free workshops to help people find the perfect pair of jeans will be on offer in the Victoria Centre, Nottingham. Liz Sewell, the centre's marketing manager said, "Jeans can be a mission impossible to shop for."

WEDNESDAY MAY 11

A NEAT WRITER, EARTH MOTHERS AND THE RED CORSET

One daily habit at 85 Danethorpe Vale was the 11am coffee. This often coincided nicely with the end of my daily writing stint. Derrick, Valerie and I would partake of the Nescafé, usually with accompanying biscuits.

Why was I comforted by this small routine? Possibly because it put me in mind of 'elevenses'. If some memories of the past were disturbing and capable of producing melancholia, others were simply bathed in a soft diffused light. 'Elevenses' was among the latter. The word 'elevenses' evoked such 1950s' morning radio period pieces on the then Light Programme, as *Workers' Playtime* or *Music While You Work*. The work/play connection was pretty strong in those days. The world was no happier or more secure then than it is now, but appeared so. 'Elevenses' also evoked the almost forgotten (though still available) *Camp Coffee* — no connection to the gay scene, but the precursor to the instant coffee revolution of Maxwell House and Nescafé. A bottle of *Camp Coffee,* whose label added the then unfathomable phrase 'With Chicory Essence', contained a mysterious dark and thick liquid, to be diluted with hot water. Nostalgia recently nudged me to buy a bottle, and the nostalgia was soon put in its place when I tasted it. Revolting. Still intact was the colonialist/imperialist label artwork, an anachronism which inspired the writer Tony Harrison to a splendid poem, "Old Soldiers" (*Collected Poems*, Penguin 2007).

Other activities at number 85 also linked more to a previous age included the daily milk deliveries, a service which had died out in many areas. Nostalgia apart, returnable milk bottles were more eco-friendly than disposable plastic milk cartons, and easier to open, so it made good sense to have milkmen (there seemed to be no milkwomen). In addition, it meant another human being calling at your door, which for many lonely isolated people was pretty important.

Secondly, Valerie was wont to tackle 500-piece jigsaws, a leisure activity I'd not seen in years. I had never once completed a jigsaw. Half-way through there was always the small voice reminding me that life was short. As the living room at number 85 boasted no proper table, jigsaw assembly required a certain ingenuity, the connected pieces balanced on a chair, or on the floor, where they risked an errant foot. I watched Valerie putting in the pieces for some time but the attraction still eluded me.

My regular chair in the living room afforded me the least advantageous view through the full-length French window of the lower back-garden patio. On this morning I sat on the settee, and realised just how much, given Valerie's habit of putting bird feed out four or five times a day, the small space resembled an aviary, with a whole variety of the feathery creatures hopping about.

"How many different types of bird come and visit?" I asked, and quick as you like Valerie replied, "Blackbirds, thrushes, starlings, wood pigeons, blue tits, great tits, goldfinch, long-tailed tits, wrens, sparrows and dunnocks." I was quietly envious, my avian knowledge being a little short of encyclopaedic once we discounted the obvious, such as knowing a golden eagle from a hummingbird.

Valerie and Derrick were also filling their newly constructed pond, carrying endless buckets of water from the kitchen up the considerable slope and steps of the garden. My suggestion for a quicker and more convenient long hose was poo-pooed. I think they enjoyed the ritual, the ceremonial labour of completing the task.

Visiting Eastwood *had* connected me to my past in unexpected ways, and I was to make another connection, with the visit to Margaret Middleton, Stanley's widow. I'd met Margaret briefly at Stanley's funeral in 2009, though

I doubted she'd remember me among all the mourners, and I don't think she did.

A small, trim woman, button-bright, she lives in the 1908 house in Caledon Road, Sherwood, a street of solid-looking respectable properties that seemed to reflect the unflamboyant world of Stanley's novels. Yet inside, the house was distinctive and memorable, just as Stanley's characters were. You walked through the front door into a circular hall up from which led a wide spiral staircase to a large circular landing with six doors leading off, looked down upon by a glass dome of a ceiling.

Throughout the house you came across examples of Stanley's accomplished oil paintings, which he somehow found time to create along with his organ-playing, his choir-singing, a life as a fulltime school teacher, and — oh yes — those 45 novels which he wrote and published at the remarkable rate of one per year.

Few novelists could have created such a body of quality writing, yet Stanley's profile remained low. His Booker Prize had come in 1973 for his novel *Holiday*, and was shared with Nadime Gordimer, a £10,000 cash award, plus a cut-glass art-deco statue of a slim woman holding aloft a tray or flat receptacle out of which you could imagine an Olympic flame surging forth.

Stanley's first novel, *A Short Answer*, was published in

Margaret Middleton

1958, my third year at High Pavement, and the couple moved into Caledon Road in 1961, the year I left the school.

Stanley Middleton's whole academic life, three years at Nottingham University apart, was spent at High Pavement School, first as a pupil, then as a teacher. Each of his 45 novels was published by Hutchinson,

195

a consistency rivalled by few if any author/publisher partnerships.

If dead French and German authors had planted one literary seed, Stanley Middleton had planted another.

In a black metal trunk in the upstairs study were stored the handwritten manuscripts of all the novels, written on lined hardback notebooks. "He would write just one draft of each novel by hand," said Margaret, "then he would ask me to look at it for any minor corrections. Then he would have it typed up ready for the publisher."

This led to another extraordinary link. The novels were typed up by Jean Dobson, the wife of Stanley's fellow English teacher, the late Ken Dobson, known affectionately to all us pupils as 'Dobbo'. Dobbo was himself a remarkable person, quietly spoken, non-authoritarian. One term he spent a full lesson a week reading out loud to us the entire novel *The Day of the Triffids* by John Wyndham, and after each session he would speak about the book's development.

There were no tests set round the book, no exams, no swotting, nor did I ever know how these sessions were supposed to fit into our official education.

Initially we lads saw this as a 'skive' period, a chance to sit back, doodle, drift off, and for some it possibly remained thus, but slowly the book drew us into its mix of adventure, sci-fi and social observation, and I'd find myself thinking about it afterwards; we even talked about it in the playground. This was not normal behaviour. What was going on? Another seed was planted.

Jean Dobson was still alive, aged 91, and was Margaret's best friend. Would I like to meet her? The sooner the better. "Stanley would leave himself a six-week gap between finishing one book and starting the next," she said, "and then he would be off again. He was a very easy man to live with as long as you realised he needed his time to write every day — usually in the morning. He hated the idea of holidays, but said he

196

wouldn't mind going to China as long as he could be back in time for tea."

I picked up the book containing the original fountain pen manuscript. The text was beautifully neat, the few alterations, where the original words were scored through with a thin straight line, done with meticulous care, and the new version written neatly above. Through the years the elegant handwriting had deteriorated hardly at all. This was the work of a creative brain whose process was all but complete before the letters were applied to the paper; what emerged was already almost the finished product.

This was rare for a writer, an unusual gift. Most of us have to thrash about on the page much more than this. Several writers, of course, work entirely on screen now, though the old school still value pen and paper in the early stages.

I contrasted Stanley's ordered manuscripts with my own handwritten early drafts, the only similarity being the use of a fountain pen. Mine were untidy scrawls, a rambling mess of random observations and descriptions later needing major surgery. I could often barely read my own words, and each page was littered with scribbled side notes, footnotes, arrows leading here and there, jottings in the margin.

And I thought of Stanley himself, knowledgeable, talented, yet the most modest of men, with a strong sense of inner calm. Since I'd left High Pavement, he was the only teacher I'd stayed in touch with. He'd written a piece for the small litmag I'd run at Sheffield University, I'd been to see him give talks on Tyneside, and — something that touched me most — he had come to Waterstones bookshop in Nottingham in 2005 for the launch of my Five Leaves poetry collection, *I Married the Angel of the North*.

And I could think of few novelists less interested in courting publicity. What was the world's least likely scenario? Stanley Middleton on a chat show.

For the second consecutive day, the life of a Nottingham writer was being revealed to me; the previous day

197

Kath Hall talking about D.H. Lawrence, today Margaret on Stanley Middleton.

"Each afternoon he would go off for his thirty-minute walk, which was when he turned things over for the next day's writing," said Margaret. "This was his pattern, and he never wanted any fuss."

"His last book was finished in 2009," she said, selecting the manuscript from the trunk. "It was called *A Cautious Approach*, and Stanley died before it was published. He had cancer of the bowel, and at the end he wanted to die. When he finished writing the book he said to me, well, that's it, no more."

"Stanley went in the retirement home in June 2009 and the next month he was dead," she continued. "It was a stressful period, as I was having a hip replacement at Woodthorpe Hospital at the same time."

That was the nearest I heard this remarkable woman come to mentioning any personal misfortune. She and Stanley were married 58 years and had two daughters. Now Margaret had grandchildren and great-grandchildren. The house retained a strong sense of Stanley Middleton without in any way being a shrine. It was light, airy, well-ordered.

A glass-fronted bookcase downstairs contained published versions of all Stanley's novels, row after impressive row. Normally only formulaic writers or Mills & Boon hacks could achieve this level of productivity.

Stanley Middleton

During our conversation, the doorbell rang. It was a young man keen to sign Margaret up to a new gas supplier. She said she wasn't interested, but the young man, no doubt desperate for the commission, persisted. I joined her on the doorstep, and between us we eventually

198

saw the pushy bloke off. "Your loss," he said grumpily and walked out of the gate. When we closed the door, we both laughed spontaneously.

Before I left, I asked Margaret in which nursing home Stanley had died.

"It was The Firs on Mansfield Road," she replied. I had good enough reason not to forget The Firs. Prior to a nursing home, it had been a maternity home. Stanley Middleton had died in the same building in which I was born.

I took my leave of Margaret, promising to return.

My publisher at Five Leaves gave me a copy of that final Stanley Middleton novel, *A Cautious Approach*, set once again in the fictional town of Beechnall, a verbal amalgam, I assume, of the Nottingham districts of Beeston and Hucknall. I'd have liked to ask Stanley why he changed the city's name, as all other local places, Mansfield, Skegness and Worksop, were given their proper identity in his work, as were separate districts of Nottingham itself. The book was published posthumously in 2010.

I thought I was familiar with the style of Stanley's writing, unsensational yet cerebral, but realised with shame how few of his books I'd actually read, and exposing myself to them now slightly shifted my perspective. His Booker Prize award in the 1970s had prompted me to read the award winner *Holiday,* set mainly in Skegness, plus one more. Why such a wretched record? By being both my schoolteacher and a writer the man had a foot in both my Nottingham and post-Nottingham lives, so why had I not kept up with his novels? I had no answer. Making up for lost time, I read three from Middleton's *oeuvre*, starting with *A Cautious Approach.* This is a hesitant love story where the words 'bodice-ripper' don't come readily to mind. The main character, George Taylor, as ordinary a name as you could get, is a former teacher in poor health. The balance of George's tentative life is upset as he is gradually drawn into a

199

series of new personal relationships, and one romantic one with Mirabel. We're four-fifths of the way through the book before we get any action there.

Middleton's characters are quiet, intelligent, and likely to spend long sessions discussing Yeats' poetry. Little happens on the surface, but emotions churn away beneath. In some sections, he uses more dialogue than any novelist I know, and the speech is fairly heightened. He may well have made a good playwright. I had to look up some of the words in the book, such as 'cynosure' (a centre of attraction), but there is no sense of an author showing off in the manner of say, Will Self.

The work is deeply unfashionable and pretty low key. That his creative energies were sustained to the end was remarkable, even if structurally *A Cautious Approach* comes over as a little odd, and a few characters seem to hang off the edge of the pages. Would Stanley Middleton's writing survive? The majority of authors splutter a little after their death and are then forgotten, and none of us could predict for sure who the survivors would be.

From Stanley's last novel, I leapfrogged back to his first. *A Short Answer* is a richly textured piece of writing, whose subtleties would have eluded the young Mortimer had I tackled it at the time of publication in 1958. Middleton emerged at the same time as Sillitoe, Barstow, Wain and the rest of the brash young working-class British novelists from the North and the Midlands who blew away literary complacency in the 50s and 60s with their stark realism and depiction of life as lived by people most previous novels had ignored.

But Stanley's books somehow slipped under the radar, his middle-class characters unfashionable and non-pyrotechnic. Their conversation was learned, albeit painfully honest, and the few working-class people in this novel come over as brusque and often unattractive. Sam Marshall, the 'hero', is a bank clerk, and the book is littered with professors, clerics, bank managers and other professional people.

200

Yet the style is extraordinary, a command of language and distinctive way with dialogue matched by few other modern writers. The following insult, delivered to our main character, is worthy of Shakespeare. "You vile creeping dung-born stinking insect," he said. "You obscene scrawler on a slimy lavatory wall. You leprous inflated bladder." Elsewhere someone is referred to memorably as 'a pudding of fire'. With its mention of football rattles, blue bags of salt in crisps, and Teddy Boys scandalously jiving at the village hall dance, *A Short Answer* is firmly of its late 50s time.

The book is informed by an early incident in which Sam has a conversation with God. When the book was first published, and my brother Alex told me this fact, I was amazed. Was this the kind of thing that happened in novels? Blimey! Sam and others attempt to come to terms with this phenomenon throughout the book, as he finds himself drifting into an affair with his friend's wife. Seeking a second godly conversation for guidance, he finds redemption in an unlikely manner and via a final small earthly miracle.

The book is intellectually demanding, but also highly entertaining. I grew fascinated with the elevated barbarous conversations, the almost total lack of small talk. And on page 54, in a book that manages to address some great issues of our time, is the least likely event imaginable — a bank robbery.

Nottingham itself is not always powerfully evoked, though in the final pages of a mainly middle-class novel, our 'hero' travels out to the Nottinghamshire pit villages, and these are described by Middleton with a power that would not have shamed Lawrence.

Stanley Middleton was among Hutchinson's 'New Authors' list in 1958. The firm had faith in him then and kept the faith for another 52 years till he died.

Reading *A Short Answer* now affected me deeply, as if not being aware of such a powerful piece of Nottingham writing for all these years was, for a fellow Nottingham writer, little short of criminal. Still, I was aware of it now, better late than never.

201

This sense of guilt hurried me to read the author's own favourite, his second novel, *Harris's Requiem*, first published by Hutchinson in 1960, but republished by Trent Editions in 2006 with a long and thoughtful introduction by David Belbin, who confessed it was his favourite Middleton novel too. My own publisher at Five Leaves was of a similar opinion. The book received sixteen reviews within a fortnight of publication (many new novels today fail to attract a single one), and in the main they were highly positive.

The eponymous Harris is a Nottingham (Beechnall) schoolmaster/composer and the requiem is for his recently dead father. Not particularly likeable or sociable, Harris strikes up prickly relationships with many characters in the book as his choral work nears its première, and he realises the chances of an artist's success or failure are often in the hands of the rich and ruthless, who pull the city's political and economic strings. In many ways the book is about how art and commerce co-exist or compete, and though the author inevitably comes down (via Harris) in support of art, there is nothing starry-eyed about such an affirmation. So keen is Middleton not to glamorise his main character that he makes mention early on of Harris's false teeth.

Other main characters include the hapless fellow-teacher Winterburn, under risk of dismissal for incompetent teaching, the hard-nosed entrepreneur and Harris's patron Cooke, and the somewhat flaky Mrs Brand who writes the requiem's libretto and is keen to seduce Harris. This doesn't happen and sex itself is mainly absent. Middleton again shows his unique talent for dialogue; it's acerbic, crotchety, often going for the jugular and quite unlike the speech in most modern novels. Interestingly, the author turned the book into a BBC Radio play in 1972.

Like a David Storey novel, *Harris's Requiem* gives a glimpse of powerful men and networks controlling most aspects of provincial industrial city life. It also conjures the life and conflicts of the 1950s' grammar school. There is a telling section based round corporal punishment, which reminded me that when the book was being written Stanley was my own English teacher at High Pavement Grammar School, and I got corporally thwacked there several times myself — though not, I hasten to add, by Stanley Middleton.

As David Belbin points out in his introduction, novels inspired by classical music are rare — Vikram Seth's *An Equal Music* is the only one I've read — and the author's profound knowledge of the subject is obvious; the soaring description of the requiem's actual performance takes the reader's breath away.

Despite its many claims to fame, I don't rate *Harris's Requiem* quite as highly as others, because the book is almost over-informed with music at the expense of other developments. Middleton tosses in such technical words as *diapason* with no explanation, and it has an over-abundance of characters, some appearing fleetingly. But the writing is challenging and deeply intelligent; I emerged from the period I spent reading these three Stanley Middleton novels as if from an ice-cold intellectual shower, a dramatically energising effect that left me wanting to abandon all conversational trivia and talk like Stanley Middleton characters. I'm probably incapable of that, but I can at least dedicate my own humble book to the man.

* * *

Sometimes the visitor to a place can spot something the long-term resident, blinded by familiarity, would miss, or take for granted. Thus I noticed how most locals simply hurried past a highly individual shop tucked away on the otherwise unprepossessing corner of Hall Street, Sherwood, a few hundred yards from the busy Mansfield Road.

The Mystic Moon was run by the proprietor Soroya Cordery with help from her brother, the visual artist Usuf

203

Choudhury, and her sister Rani. How best to describe *The Mystic Moon?* It is a shrine to witchcraft, wicca, and paganism, a psychedelically fronted shop (painted by Usuf) which runs workshops in reiki, crystal healing, hypnotherapy, cosmic ordering and the study of angels. Soroya herself is a spiritualist and the shop's name came to her in a dream, ("If you mention it, don't forget the definite article," she said. "That's important.") It was a clutter of the exotic and the unexpected, a cornucopia of the alternative and the spiritualist. Sherwood of another age and culture to my own upbringing, yet there was a link.

The family's father, Mohamed Lucknan Uddin had founded the Koh-in-Nor restaurant on Alfreton Road. This was back in the 1950s, Nottingham's very first Indian restaurant and a place of great curiosity. I remember asking my parents, what *is* an Indian restaurant ? I had little idea. Nor they, as I recall. Curry was an

The Mystic Moon — a cornucopia of the alternative and the spiritual

Usuf Choudhury — artist

exotic foreign dish few on Sherwood Estate would ever have tasted. According to Usuf, initially the restaurant's main customers were ex-servicemen who had spent time in India, but often several nights would go by with no diners turning up.

"We lived in West Bridgford [a suburb just south of the River Trent], the first non-whites to do so," said Soroya, "and a lot of people didn't want us there. Generally people are more tolerant now, and they are also more tolerant towards the shop."

Hang on. Usuf was only 30 years old now. And his dad ran the restaurant 60 years ago?

It was true. Usuf's father married his mother when she was 16, and he was 60. They were Bangladeshis and it was an arranged marriage. The father had died almost a quarter of a century before, in 1987, though his mother was still alive, and still only in her 50s.

Soroya described herself as a wiccan spiritualist earth mother — a species thin on the ground in Sherwood, or

205

anywhere else come to that. "What we teach is generally less harmful than other religions," she said. "People expect us to be devil worshippers. We don't even believe in the devil — that's a Christian concept."

I returned to Danethorpe Vale. Valerie had been working on the new pond, and was relaxing with a jigsaw. She was playing *Simply Red* on a small CD player hidden away in a corner. The music changed the entire atmosphere of the living room, so much so, that in the opposite corner, the TV set, used to all the attention, had gone into a major sulk.

* * *

My love of and dedication to live theatre was such that I would go to see any play, anywhere, any time. This addiction embraced writing plays, directing plays, devising plays, watching plays and occasionally acting in plays. Nor was a play itself essential. I could quite happily sit in an empty theatre and indulge a kind of theatrical meditation until thrown out by the caretaker.

In my one month's return to Nottingham, I was to see more live plays than I had done in my initial twenty-one years in the city. And when I came across a reference to a new theatre, visiting it *asap* became a priority. Thus The Lace Market Theatre, which did its best to hide away in Halifax Place. The secretive strategy included having a small frontage which could easily have been that of an estate agent's offices, and being down a no-through road where nobody wandered. Halifax Place led off Pilcher Gate which itself had no bars or restaurants, and was dominated one side by a multi-storey car park. But most cunning of all, the theatre had buried its auditorium underground. All these attempts to hide away proved abortive. I found it, as did a large audience — only ten of the 118 seats that evening were unoccupied.

Much of Nottingham's Lace Market was a commercial centre reminiscent of the City of London in that away from office hours, the streets were deserted. Other parts were given over to new bars and restaurants. There was now no sign of lace, once one of the city's most famous products, but among the Lace Market's streets were a few gems and The Lace Market Theatre was one of them.

It is an amateur company that had bought the present premises for £5,800 in 1970, since when it has spent more than £60,000 of its own money adapting and converting them. You entered the main door then went either downstairs to the theatre or upstairs to the spacious bar/coffee rooms, whose vaulted roof had impressively broad beams. Sherwood oak, I assumed.

The company has 350 members and according to committee man Dave Nightingale (who was selling the interval ice-cream that night), it can call on more than 100 adult actors as well as an active youth theatre.

In a recession, with professional theatre tickets often in excess of £50, good quality amateur theatre has an opportunity to make its mark. The fact that much of the amateur theatre world is conservative and over-cautious puts some people off, and the very phrase 'amateur theatre' suggests well-intentioned muddlers and Hooray Henrys. If you play rock music you are a rock musician full stop, and no-one puts the tag 'amateur' or 'professional' in front of your band. Theatre is different, and of course more middle-class.

The Lace Market Theatre is far from cautious in its programming; the season included Joe Orton's black-humoured *Loot*, Lorca's poetic masterpiece *Blood Wedding*, Kafka's *The Trial* (the Steven Berkoff version done by Nottingham Playhouse), Brian Friel's *Dancing at Lughnasa* and Anthony Burgess's controversial *A Clockwork Orange*.

That night's offering was *Dinner* by Moira Buffini. I'd never heard of the play, nor the writer. It had echoes of Orton and a hint of J.B. Priestley's *An Inspector Calls*.

Dinner was a darkly mysterious play about the dinner party from hell, where Kareena Sims played Paige, the

207

anti-heroine/dinner hostess cruelly stripping away her guests' defences as she employed her deadly word games. The actor wore the most arresting red corset you were ever likely to see in the East Midlands, and had the eye make-up of a panda.

The production played for seven nights and was among an impressive programme of fourteen productions in a year. Graeme Jennings' spirited direction included one scene where the butler was called upon to serve each dinner guest with a live lobster.

The six-page programme contained not a word about the author or her work, so I looked her up. Moira Buffini is an English writer of Irish parents born in 1965, and had been described as a 'metaphysical playwright', whatever that might mean. She adapted *Jane Eyre* for the BBC, and her plays are all published by Faber.

Despite being hidden away, The Lace Market Theatre, unlike several modern theatres, opens its daytime doors to the public from Monday to Friday, when the duty officer is happy to show people round. Worth the trip.

THIS NOTTINGHAM

Skegness and Hand-Knitted Swimming Costumes will be the subjects at a history society meeting. The event will take place at Maycliffe Hall, Toton Lane Stapleford at 7.30pm. Admission is £1.50.

THURSDAY MAY 12

SISTER SALT, THE NON-WHISTLING GROCER, AND THE SHOUTING OF LANG LANG

Not crossing the threshold of 97 Danethorpe Vale, which I now accepted was the only plausible reality, was likely to have a major influence on the nature of this book. To have entered that house would have released a tsunami of memory and detail. To be denied it brought a certain sadness. But such a tsunami may well have swamped the writing.

What was now emerging was at arms-length from my upbringing, just as I was often at arms-length from my family when growing up on Sherwood Estate. And there was the constant juggling of the past and the present, and the fact that I quarry my own past usually much less than many authors, at least directly. What slowly became clear was how the present was nudging away the past. If we took the metaphor of a football game's territorial advantage, I had expected this to be seventy-five per cent past, twenty-five per cent present. But the present had the upper hand. Having said which, at times the past came thudding back.

I woke this morning thinking of my father, and how he would shave in freshly boiled water. Many times I had tried to emulate this, and on each occasion the attempt was scaldingly painful and quickly abandoned. What was his secret? And why had I never asked?

Two quotations follow. A prize for anyone who can recognise either.

'September sunshine splashed the waxed polished table-top. There was a little modest silver to be seen and a bowl of early chrysanthemums.'

209

'He stood breathless. The world's happiest man. Or so he would have claimed.'

Between these two quotations lay a half century of a writer's output, a lifetime of creativity. The first was the opening paragraph of Stanley Middleton's first book *A Short Answer*, the second the closing sentences of his final novel *A Cautious Approach*. Between these two extracts was a timespan not dissimilar to that covered by my leaving Sherwood Estate and now returning, a long journey, an adventure of countless places, people and experiences.

I could now place the first book's opening next to the final book's ending without effort. This in a way was time travel, a temporal juggling. What did time care? It meant nothing to time. Time itself was interested only in the present. The rest was either dead, the past, or not yet born, the future, neither worth much attention to time which devoted all its energy to the present moment. How simple a concept this was. How difficult to carry through.

Was that final Stanley Middleton sentence prophetic? It may be ludicrous to suggest a man dying of bowel cancer could be happy, yet in the sense that he knew his job as a writer was complete, it may have been true. Or again, at that final moment, a half-century of writing may have meant nothing.

I was growing fond of both the people and the building at The Place, Sherwood's resource centre, tucked away down Melrose Street off Mansfield Road. The less corporate a place, the less talk about a market-driven 'product', the fewer consultants I could see hovering in doorways, the more I liked it.

The Place was OK. Though smaller, it reminded me of The Linskill Centre in North Shields, the home of our theatre company Cloud Nine and other small arts and crafts organisations. Many of us had fought hard to ensure Linskill's survival in the face of a Tory council plan to demolish it for luxury flats, and its future now looked safe.

I cycled up to The Place that morning with no particular plan. Jane Gill introduced me to Rita Dobbins of the recently formed craft group. The group thus far had only four members, but as Rita said, "Our art group started with four not long ago, and now it's up to fourteen."

Rita was the driving force behind the recent Sherwood Arts Week. She made her own jewellery, and called her business *One Melted Moment*. How come?

"All my jewellery is crystal and that's what it takes to create crystal."

The jewellery embraced emerald, ruby, turquoise, topaz, jade, hematite, and one which sounded like a zesty drink, citrine.

Rita was sixty-five, and since 1974 had lived at the far end of Costock Avenue, a thoroughfare with an ambivalent relationship to Sherwood Estate. Costock's west end consisted of private detached houses with bay windows, whereas the east end had been built as council houses, a fact which left it with a certain schizophrenia, unsure of its relationship to the estate itself.

My own contact with Costock Avenue was twofold. I delivered Co-op groceries there, and my father, when he became a car owner, rented a Costock Avenue garage. There were no garages on the estate proper, nor that many cars parked on the streets. The garage was attached to a house belonging to a woman called Sister Salt, who was in charge of Nightingale 11, the ward on which my mother worked at Nottingham City Hospital.

Sister Salt (as she was referred to, even outside the hospital) was small in stature, stiff-backed, and with a surface formality that put the fear of God into you. Her eyes drilled through you from behind round spectacles, she spoke in clipped sentences, and her presence made you feel guilty without a clue as to what you were guilty of.

Sister Salt — the words sounded like the name of a band — did nothing as mundane as cough, scratch her nose, or break into laughter. I was partly afraid of her, but partly

211

fascinated. Was she beyond mere mortal emotion? Did she exist on another plane entirely? On rare occasions, a small smile would come to Sister Salt's lips. It was akin to seeing a statue smile, and at such moments, I was both thrilled and disappointed, as if part of me wanted her to be human, and part of me wanted something else.

After I'd described Sister Salt to Rita Dobbins, she said, "That's the same house as mine. I bought it off Sister Salt."

There was more. Opposite the western end of Costock Avenue I remembered the tiny cobblers shop called Gamble's. It was so small, size eight were the biggest shoes they could take in for repair, (not strictly true, but indulge me). Such was the intoxicating smell of leather once you opened the door into this tiny universe, that my ambition was to work there, indeed live there. Unfortunately after five minutes in the shop, the sweet aroma mysteriously disappeared, and so did the ambition.

The shop was originally run by old man Gamble, a gnomelike man with no chin. Later he retired, and the business was taken over by his son, who was taller, but of similar reduced chinnage. I wondered if he would slowly shrink in height with the passage of time.

"The son's name was Ian," said Rita, "And I would spend many an hour in that shop just chatting to him. I was very fond of him."

Really? How fond?

"Just fond."

The premises are now a flower shop.

Rita also remembered the Co-op in its previous form. The red-brick building was then split into three separate units, grocery, greengrocery and butcher's. I worked as delivery boy in the grocery where the manager was a young man called Maurice, one of the few people I knew who was unable to whistle.

"Go on Maurice, whistle *Singing in the Rain*," we delivery lads would taunt, or "Have a bash at *The*

212

Runaway Train, go on." Maurice would curse, and cuff us round the head.

Educating Rita Dobbins had been an interesting process. She'd attended Manning Girls' School next to The Forest, the only all-girls school in Nottingham (now relocated to Aspley) and the sister school to my own High Pavement Grammar.

"I was a very bright girl, and the only one from our group to pass the 11-plus, which proved socially divisive." This rang a bell.

"I read *Pilgrim's Progress* at the age of seven and when I was eleven my mum bought me a set of encyclopaedias."

And all this despite terrible handicaps.

"I was left-handed but, for a whole year from the age of four, at Bilsthorpe Primary School, my teacher tied my left hand behind my back, and forced me to write with my right hand, which I do to this day, but my hand-writing is terrible."

The child of a single parent, then quite a rarity, Rita suffered the stigma of the infamous purple dinner tickets, which signified children from disadvantaged, impover-ished homes. You may as well have stuck the children in a corner with a giant arrow bearing the word INFERIOR! pointed at them. The tickets exposed the recipients to the cruel taunting of other children.

Her recall of school lacked any nostalgia. "I hated it," she said. "Any attempt at creative individuality was stamped on at the expense of a strict formality. My mother eventually paid £15 to take me out at the age of fourteen."

Rita went to college of her own volition while bringing up a brain-damaged child, and now she is flowering as an artist in crystal jewellery.

A name cropping up frequently was Peter Mansfield, Sherwood's Neighbourhood Action officer. I visited Peter briefly in his spacious offices above Sherwood Police Station in Mansfield Road, the old Lloyds Bank site. He was surrounded by empty desks, government cuts meaning there were no bodies to occupy them. Peter told me Sherwood Estate's popularity had seen it replace Clifton Estate as the city's longest waiting list for would-be tenants — more than 100.

At one moment his eyes lit up, as he spoke with great enthusiasm about the area and its achievements: how local people raised £60,000 to build the new multi-sports Jason Spencer area, in the memory of the young man whose name I had seen all those weeks ago on the sub-station fence, how crime in Sherwood was down, and how it now had the annual festival, the street market, the arts week.

At the next moment the light in those eyes flickered and all but went out.

"But this job's not the same for me anymore. I need a change. I retire on March 2, 2013. I'm ready for it."

Another flicker and the light was back.

"I'm helping develop St. Ann's allotments now. They're reputed to be the biggest in Europe — 500 separate plots! Come and see them."

I never did. Nor, in such a short space of time, had I ever met a man displaying such a contrasting combination of the zealous and the world-weary. I left Peter Mansfield among his sea of empty desks, already thinking about him as a character in a future play.

That evening Nottingham Forest were playing the first leg of their championship play-off semi-final at the City Ground against Swansea City. This was a must-see game that I couldn't see, having already bought tickets, along with Derrick and Valerie, for the concert by the Chinese pianist and modern phenomenon, Lang Lang, so good they named him twice.

Lang Lang, rather like Nigel Kennedy two decades previously, had opened up classical music to a newer younger generation who would previously have found its stuffy elitist reputation mystifying and off-putting. In his publicity shot at the piano he was wearing Adidas trainers, which may have been product placement. When he walked

214

on stage at the Royal Concert Hall he had on more tradi-tional black patent-leather shoes, though he declined the usual bow tie in favour of an open-necked shirt.

The rise of Lang Lang's popularity had seen forty million young people in China take up the classical piano. In Britain I personally knew two people in the same cate-gory.

The hall was packed, much of the younger audience unaware of classical music's conventions. This led to great fun. Some people broke into applause between movements (which always seemed more celebratory than the repressed silence and occasional coughs we are usually asked to indulge). People were texting on their mobiles, and using the same mobiles to take photographs and videos.

One convention was that classical pianists did not talk to the audience. A stiff bow was usually the only acknowl-edgement of their existence. I quite liked this. It added to the mystique. But how would the custom survive in the age of celebrity, when tittle-tattle was placed higher in the pecking order than talent, and chat shows and celeb mags fed us a non-stop diet of trivial information on the famous? Would Lang Lang end up on *Celebrity Big Bother*? Would he engage in idle banter?

No idle banter. We did get a brief communiqué, which came at the end of the advertised programme, as the audience clapped and cheered for an encore. Lang Lang cupped his hand to his mouth and shouted "I'll do a Chopin étude!" and followed this by a short bit of Schumann, then off.

There was a certain restlessness to the audience. The programme — by Beethoven, Prokofiev, and Albéniz — wasn't overfamilar stuff, so the sense, especially among those who looked to be classical first-timers, was rather like someone listening to Radio 3 for the first time. But then, there was a first time for everything.

Lang Lang, like all great artists, created his own universe, one which dissolved as we emerged into the bustling city centre. Yet what was this underlying sense of deflation? Why so many gloomy faces from people sporting red and white scarves? Nottingham Forest, hot favourites to win the match, had managed only a 0-0 draw, meaning that in the return leg at Swansea, they had a mountain to climb. I think that's the right cliché.

THIS NOTTINGHAM

Bird breeding seasons are being disturbed by people playing bird song noises on their mobile phones. Staff at Attenborough Nature Reserve say wildlife photographers were making the noises to lure birds off their nests.

FRIDAY MAY 13

MONKEY TREE MEMORIES
AS THE MOVING HAND WRITES,
AND MOVES ON

Still lying on the bed when I woke was a copy of the previous day's *Nottingham Post*. On the back page were the confident pre-match words of the Forest manager Billy Davies. Nothing could date so fast, nor sound so hollow in the light of eventual experience as these managerial pronouncements. Davies was confident Forest would beat Swansea, go on to Wembley and achieve premier league status.

None of these happened, and soon after, Billy Davies was sacked.

Football managers were our modern shamen. We clung to their every predictive word, as if delivered from on high. We invested in football managers' non-existent magical powers in the belief this would ensure our own team's success. When they spoke, we lent managers' thoughts the gravitas and wisdom of a Delphic oracle, whereas they were often the hastily cobbled together sentences of an overstressed, pressurised, individual.

No matter how many times such belief was shown to be false, no matter on how many occasions their words proved to be empty, we awaited once more their mystical pronouncements on the coming fixture against West Bromwich Albion. "We shall win," said the shaman, and we would shake our spears in noisy affirmation. We desperately need a messiah. Politicians have failed us. Our religious leaders have failed us. Our celebrities, like a Chinese take-away, gave us but fleeting sustenance. Who else do we have? Simon Cowell? Alan Sugar?

So we plump for the blotchy-faced, paunchy, over-weight chewers of gum to lead us to the promised land.

That for ninety per cent of the time they would lead us into the wilderness fails to deter us. This time it would all be different. This time the programme notes would speak true.

One of my books for children is called *Utter Nonsense*, a collection of silly poems illustrated by Geoff Laws. I mention this not as an unashamed plug to bolster sales (much though they need it), but for the fact that in the biog notes of that collection is the following: *The author once won a prize at Seely Infant School in Nottingham for blowing out candles.*

This is only partly true. I did attend Seely Infant School, but there was no prize for blowing out candles. Other parts of the biog notes *were* true. For instance: *He has successfully predicted clouds since 1967.*

And now, late in the day in my Nottingham return, I decided to revisit those premises I last set foot in almost 60 years previously. The decision took me by surprise. Seely Infant School was at the far end of such a long dark tunnel as almost to be in another galaxy. More mixed metaphors. What did I hope to achieve by this retro action?

I had no idea. On impulse I rang the school, and after being passed to various people, spoke to the head teacher Sally Clark. Men of a certain age ringing to gain access to infant schools were naturally viewed with a certain suspicion. But eventually I persuaded the school that my credentials were genuine and the visit was sanctioned.

Seely School, at the west end of the estate on Edingley Square, and only a jemmy's throw away from Sherwood Prison, was built in 1925 as part of the Sherwood Council Estate Development. It now had 210 pupils aged 3–7, and 80 nursery pupils. Those who remembered the old school gates would get a shock to see modern realities.

The school is ringed with high metal security-fencing, while CCTV cameras fix their cold eyes on visitors, who can gain entrance only via an intercom system. The world has become a more frightened place with our prison-like

218

schools, our gated homes, our high security town centres where our every move is observed.

And as is the way of things, we feel less, not more safe.

Teaching in the 21st century is among the most stressful occupations known. I accept investment banking is stressful, but teaching serves some useful purpose. I have seen many teachers burnt out, cynical, suffering massive depressions or otherwise defeated at an early age.

Sally Clarke, Head of Seely School

I have worked a good deal as a writer in schools with contrasting fortunes. Some schools are bliss, with a sense of charged excitement as the young minds take on creative challenges. Other schools are pure hell, the staff seeing out time, the kids sullen, resentful, and for me, only the knowledge that, unlike everyone else, I could escape at 3.30pm guaranteeing I survive the day. Schools are not meant to be battlegrounds.

And while the system is often at the mercy of Education Ministers deeply ignorant of the true potential and meaning of the very word education, the attitude of any head teacher is also highly influential, and soaks itself into the fabric of a school. Invariably a flexible, compassionate, confident and hands-on head means you are in for an interesting

219

and enjoyable journey with the children. Likewise the reverse.

Sally Clarke was unusual. For the last 15 years she had job-shared with her colleague Jacqui Newton, the last six as head at Seely. And despite the spirit-sapping views of the security fences, the CCTV cameras, the inside of Seely School was bright, colourful, the classrooms full of decorations and things the children had made. How bubbly these children seemed, how strong an antidote to what often lay beyond those metal fences. Sally was bright too, colourful and bubbly. Did she like the job?

"I love it! I love it!" she said with the kind of enthusiasm not often shown by a species (head teachers) usually more given to circumspection.

"Sherwood is a really interesting mix," she added. "Just consider this. It has some of the most expensive houses in Nottingham, and also Europe's highest rates of teenage pregnancy. Quite a combination."

She took time out to lead me through every classroom, introducing me to the children, though what they made of this strange gadgie I was unsure. She explained how Seely was a fully inclusive school, taking children of all abilities and disabilities, including those who would normally be siphoned off to special schools.

In the main corridor were some giant cardboard and paper heads, instantly recognisable as Roald Dahl's *BFG*. The children had made the heads for the Nottingham Playhouse Christmas pantomime in 2009. This was an imaginative way of involving young people in theatre — the pupils went to see the show they had helped create — and contrasted with my own abortive school visits to the old Playhouse, mentioned previously.

Good stuff, yet I was still unconnected, I was still unable to transpose myself to that child who walked into this school at the age of five, tightly clutching my mother's hand, and cried when she prised it loose, the same child who in the first weeks went missing and was found by his older brother in the toilets in a state of distress, vainly attempting to put back his braces, the same child who smelt the lemony aroma of the wooden parquet flooring in the main hall as he lay on his stomach for gym classes, and could smell it to this day, though the floor, I noted, had been resurfaced.

Vaguely in my memory were those same distinctive full-length wooden french windows of the classrooms, which had survived sixty years but were soon to be replaced by PVC facsimiles. These were unusual; the school culture of that time believed windows had to be built high to prevent pupils staring out and losing concentration.

Then two things jolted me back, grabbed the scruff of my neck and hurled me through more than half a century. Firstly, there was the monkey puzzle tree, planted when the school was built. Dark, mysterious and painful to the touch, the tree always slightly disturbed me, and it disturbed me initially as I looked upon it now. Yet the sense of disturbance quickly passed, replaced by something more accommodating. All my life, through everything that had happened, this tree had been here in this spot, day after day, year after year, generations of children passing through the school.

Secondly, as I walked into Classroom 5, I pulled up short. "This was it," I said, "This was my first classroom." In appearance it was little different to the other classrooms. The heavy old desks, with an inkwell at the top right-hand corner and the sturdy hinged tops had been replaced by more prosaic tables. The décor was more modern. But I knew.

The sunlight was filtering through the window just as it had then. Motes were dancing in the sunbeams, seemingly unchanged. And one moment came vividly to mind.

Aged five and six, we had recently returned from the Christmas holidays. A new year was upon us. And the instruction came from the teacher, Miss Cunningham. Novices though we still were at this activity, we were to write the new year at the top corner of the lined paper in front of us. Carefully I dipped the simple wooden pen into the inkwell, checking I left no hidden bubble of ink at the rear of the nib which would cause a splodge on the page.

Slowly, no doubt with a face screwed to concentration, I wrote the four numbers on the right side of the top right line. To a faint scratchy sound, negotiating each curve, each right angle, each cross stroke, each placement of the nib, I committed the four shapes to paper, my first memory of creating a formation of angles and curves which would communicate to other people. My first memory of being a writer.

The shapes were a number one, a nine, a four, and a second nine — the year 1949, a year so far distant as to be almost out of reach. The recall made me realise I had become part of history, even as I moved and breathed in that same room, even as I stared at the fresh young faces of the children. What did those children know of this room sixty years ago? Why should they? It was as far back to them as some Egyptian mummy.

Nineteen forty nine... Had I really written those four numbers? And what of the class's other children? Where were they now? I yearned for them to be still the same, wide-eyed, full of laughter, mainly innocent of the world which awaited them.

I was older than I recognised. Like it or not, rage as I might, and do, against the dying of the light, I was slipping into old age. But what was old age except another tiny step in history? Today had brought home a simple truth; 'history' was not something abstracted in books and disconnected from our own lives. History *was* us, real, living, we made it with our every breath, we laid down its pattern and its shape for future generations to examine.

For you, this may be self-evident. For me, it took this return to Seely School, this bridging of the almost lifelong gap between two experiences to bring it home. It took a monkey tree, and the memory of that scratchy pen. I had never truly exorcised that sense of history instilled from school; that it was something else, somewhere else, other people. Yet it was there in that classroom, that moment. And I was a part of it.

I thanked Sally Clarke for her time, gave her a copy of the book which mentioned Seely School in the biog notes, and hurried away.

Later that day I was moved to revisit Stanley Middleton's widow Margaret, with whom I felt an affinity, and not only because of her high quality cups of tea. The bonus on this visit was also to meet up with Jean Dobson, the widow of Ken 'Dobbo' Dobson, whose highly unofficial *Day of the Triffids* reading was such an important landmark in those often painful days at High Pavement Grammar School.

Jean was 91, but equally as bright and entertaining as Margaret.

"Stanley and Ken," she told me, "were always in unspoken competition as to which of them was the worst-dressed teacher in the school."

I thought back, and had to admit it was a close-run thing.

Meeting Margaret and Jean, and seeing Stanley's excellent and intricate drawing of the old High Pavement School, led me that afternoon to cycle to the Old Basford area to view the building for the first time since 1958.

Ironically, its successor, the Bestwood High Pavement School building, built in 1956, had been bulldozed to the ground, while this impressively monstrous red-brick Victorian edifice in Stanley Road looked good for several more centuries. With its endless windows, its many towers and turrets, its hidden corners and unpredictable angles, the building put me in mind of Mervyn Peake's Gormenghast Castle. It was a gloriously eccentric and imposing piece of public architecture the like of which would not be built today.

It now served as Berridge Adult Education Centre in the middle of a multi-racial area which boasted its own

223

Stanley Middleton's drawing of High Pavement School, like Gormenghast Castle

mosques, halal shops and Pakistani Community Centre. The district is also home to such idiosyncratic small retail outlets as the Screaming Carrot Vegetarian Bakery.

I had spent one year's schooling at this building. We boys — the school was all-male — would trudge the few hundred yards to a 'canteen' in Palm Street for school

The uniquely-named Screaming Carrot Vegetarian Bakery

dinners, which I recall as being a dark Dickensian edifice. It had since been demolished to make way for a small industrial estate. Also gone was the pungent hoppy smell of Shipstone's Brewery. This smell pervades my every memory of that first High Pavement year, a less than savoury aroma that on the short journey to Palm Street was often enough to dull the appetite.

That first year at a grammar school was mainly a terrifying experience. I knew few other boys, as my friends had gone to Claremont Secondary Modern. From being in the top layer at the previous school, I was now at the bottom. Most of the teachers were forbidding and remote, as were many of the older boys. My only answer to this fear was to become a boxer and knock six bells out of several opponents *en route* to becoming the school champion. In the ring, I could beat them all.

Cycling back to Danethorpe Vale — and today's cycle of several miles had included only a few inches of flat terrain — I was taken aback to whiz past a pub which I had put out of my mind.

This was partly because The Quorn, on Hucknall Road by the junction with Haydn Road, had not been a regular watering hole, partly because now it had been revamped and renamed The Hub in search of the yoof market, and partly because its main memory was one I chose not to over-indulge.

I hadn't long since started at Sheffield University, the year was 1965, when I received a letter from my former Sherwood girlfriend. I say former, as the relationship was all but over. Like many others it failed to survive the rapid changes brought about by a new student life away from home. She had visited me just the once in Sheffield and soon after wrote to say she was pregnant, and I was the father. I was summoned to meet her father on a Sunday night in The Quorn. I travelled down the thirty-five miles for probably the least sociable drink of my life.

There was a sense of Victorian melodrama about that

225

meeting, a high moral tone response which today's generation might find difficult to believe.

"I have just one question," her father said, as we sat down with our pints, "Were you intending to marry my daughter?"

"Well, no, I mean, we'd just about finished and — "

He held up his hand to silence me.

"Then you will never contact her again. Nor ever see the baby."

After which we both drank up and I returned to Sheffield. Soon afterwards their family upped sticks and moved south. The baby was born, and, as I understand, adopted. I have no idea of the name, nor even the sex. If some day, knocking on my door comes a middle-aged man or woman with the words, "Hello Dad," I shall have to deal with it.

Had I known one single fact about the child, I would have lost the protection of it being an abstraction. Had some tiny morsel of information filtered through to me over the years, all would have changed. Nothing did, and because of this, when people asked if I was haunted by the experience, I would answer no. Occasionally sad, but all consequences had been kept at one remove.

The day had churned up the past more than most. A relief then to witness an amusing and touching diversion back at 85 Danethorpe Vale.

Valerie drove up to Sherwood after we decided on an Indian takeaway for tea, though Derrick plumped for fish and chips. By this time the rain was bucketing down, and Derrick positioned himself by the open front door waiting for Valerie's return. When the car drew up, he opened his brolly, ran down to the gate and escorted Valerie back up the splashing path, the two of them laughing like — well, like drains.

For an entire month Valerie and Derrick had made me a natural part of their home. Their house was an oasis, its interior unburdened with history, or at least mine. Once outside, on the estate itself, I felt increasingly ill at ease, as if Sherwood Estate held me in some tortuous and nega-

226

tive time trap I was unable to deal with. The front door of number 85 became a portal through which I hurtled either back or forwards half a century, depending on whether I was entering or exiting the house.

For these reasons I spent less and less time on the estate, and sought sense and relief in things that defined the present, as against the previous version of Peter Mortimer. Such as theatre.

I returned to Nottingham Playhouse that night to catch Henrik Ibsen's little-known play, *The League of Youth,* adapted by the prolific Nottingham dramatist Andy Barrett, and directed by Giles Croft.

Unlike much of Ibsen, this play about political ambition and opportunism, which had never seen a full performance in the UK, was quite funny. It was even, peculiarly for Ibsen, advertised as 'a comedy'. Croft and Barrett — which could have been the name of a health food shop — had wrung extra humour and satire from the piece by making the 19th century Norwegian political scene relevant to our current coalition, the parallels at times drawn so effectively as to make the audience gasp.

Why did I so much love the experience of live theatre, and prefer seeing a play to a film, despite the latter's vastly superior technical abilities? I loved film too, but it lacked that intoxicating combination: that on one hand you may be witness to brilliant acting, inspired directing and elevated writing, while on the other, you might just see someone fall off the stage.

THIS NOTTINGHAM

FOR SALE: Hair piece. Fits over top of head. Medium ash blonde. Cost £55. Never worn! £20.

SATURDAY MAY 14

BLOWN AWAY BY THE MARKET
AND THOSE THEATRICAL VICARS

Each day I found myself studying the Nottingham A–Z, something which in twenty-one years living in the city I had failed even once to do. I could recall no instance of poring over a map of Sherwood Estate, nor linking methodically or cartographically one part of the city with another. We simply lived in this bit, and sometimes we went to other bits. And I assumed I knew all those bits. Hadn't I walked home often enough late night from Aspley or Bestwood, or Bulwell? But this current map-gazing emphasised the geographical ignorances about my native city. Could I pinpoint Attenborough, Cotgrave, or Rushcliffe?

My knowledge of several Nottingham areas was hazy. On Sherwood Estate none of us had motors, and our universe was small, with little incentive or wherewithal to broaden it out.

Only now, all these years on, and when the knowledge was mainly academic, could I hold in my head a geographical sense of Nottingham in its entirety.

Yet your own native city is unlike any other. To have grown up in a city gives you a sense of intimacy and exclusivity denied any incomer. I have spent much longer on Tyneside than I had in Nottingham. Tyneside is now my adopted home. I am better informed about the region than I ever was about Nottingham. I did not expect nor desire to move. But I was not born there.

My speech and accent were not that of Tyneside. In Nottingham, for the first time in more than forty years, I was spending extended time among people whose accent was similar to my own. And while having the same accent did not necessarily unite people, to have a different accent to those around you automatically brought a slight sense of 'otherness'. This was particularly true of Tyneside with its fierce sense of regional identity, but was relevant in Nottingham too. The fact I unthinkingly heightened my accent here (or this being Nottingham, flattened it) was simply more proof of a desire for acceptance.

I had not been forged in the furnace of Tyneside, but that of Nottingham. Nottingham made me, yet ironically, when I left it, I was still unmade. Which was perhaps the main reason we left anywhere.

It was my final weekend, and today was Sherwood Market day. A recent innovation, the street market stretched the length of the Mansfield Road hill. How ironic that after a month of almost unbroken sunshine and warm clement weather, this should prove to be the coldest and windiest day of the season, so that Mansfield Road itself had turned into a wind tunnel, the dozen or so stallholders shivering and blown about, their flimsy stall coverings billowing out like parachute silk.

Rachel Ainley's *Made in Sherwood* stall offered a range of home-made artistic felt creations, brooches, tea cosies, and flowers. A slightly trembling accordionist was doing her bit to jolly everyone up, as was the brightly dressed balloon lady, who managed to twist her inflated creations into all manner of animal shapes for children, at the risk of them blowing away (the balloons not the children, though given the wind, this was a possibility too).

These activities took place near the top of Mansfield Road. The bottom was cementing its reputation for being the more neglected area, for though drumming and other workshops were advertised in the library vicinity, nothing was happening. The Festival needed sturdier stalls, it needed more street activities, more music. But these were early days, and there was a sense of Sherwood re-inventing itself, looking for a character it had lacked in my day.

Sherwood offered live theatre that evening too. The Reformed Players staged a brace of shows a year in the

Hall of the United Reform Church behind The Sherwood Manor, and their new production was *Pools' Paradise*, a play by Philip King, directed by Sue Hall.

Here was a totally different theatrical culture. Tickets cost £4, which included tea or coffee, there were raffle tickets at £1 a strip, and looking at the number of prizes (about 25) compared to the number of audience (about 70), I estimated the odds of success were pretty high. I estimated right, and won a pocket calculator, which I have yet to use.

The audience were mainly white and of a certain age.

One problem with many of these traditional am-dram companies (as with other grassroots organisations) is in attracting the young, who are too busy social (or anti-social) networking to bother about strutting the boards with a load of old fogeys. So that the two characters referred to in the cast list as 'The Girl' and her 'Young Man' were probably within sight of the pension. Men are also a problem. Past the age of forty, the male of the species tend to go into terminal decline, recreation coming only via the pub or the football match or in such isolated leisure pursuits as fishing, sailing model boats or digging an allotment. They are not creatively social animals, and activities such as amateur dramatics are left mainly to the females of the species. The drama publisher Samuel French Ltd brought out a whole range of amateur dramatic plays with all-female casts. None for all-male.

Pools' Paradise was a play with a silly plot. Set in a vicarage, it involved the efforts of the vicar's wife to disguise the fact that her small social group had won a quarter of a million pounds on the football pools. Does anyone still play the football pools? Her husband, the vicar, was fiercely anti-gambling, so — gosh — the secret must not get out.

People over-reacted, galumphed around the stage hiding in cupboards, tripping up over chairs, and one character's main comic trait was to stutter. The play had

230

virtually no social, historical or political hinterland or intellectual ambition, its sole motive being to keep us mildly amused, which occasionally it did. It was the kind of stage piece that would forever be ignored by serious drama critics, which may or may not be important. Like many a Chinese take-away, *Pools' Paradise* was moderately pleasant for a short time, soon after which you'd forgotten you'd ever digested it.

On the plus side, in an age of increasing isolation the play brought out of their houses on three consecutive nights, groups of 60-70 people observing their fellow human beings in the age-old craft of acting out stories, and these people also used that occasion for social interaction. If for this reason alone, it was important.

Walking home through the estate that night I realised that The Five Ways had now slipped out of my life, slunk away with barely a whimper. And I no longer stood outside 97 Danethorpe Vale, staring at my sealed past. There was a loosening of the knots, a letting go, and with it a sense of inevitability, and also of sadness.

And two lime fruits still in my bag.

THIS NOTTINGHAM

POOL LEAGUE REPORT: Mad Rabbit had a walkover against Beechdale Super 7s. League Champions Colonel Burnaby cruised to an 8–2 away win against Whitemoor Numptys.

SUNDAY MAY 15

CHEESE SANDWICH BANQUETS AND OTHER MORTIMER IDIOSYNCRACIES

My time on the estate was coming to an end. I knew that not stepping over the threshold of 97 Danethorpe Vale had changed the nature of this book. I had expected the house of my upbringing to loom large. Here was the core of my Sherwood Estate existence, the place to which, for all those years, I retreated every night, and from which, every new day, I exited to face the world. To be so near and yet so far was at times unsettling, like the glimpse of a past lover in the crowd, but a glimpse and then gone. Not entering that house had meant a smaller profile to the Mortimer family than would otherwise have been the case. My childhood domestic world loomed less large. If this had initially troubled me, it did less so as I took stock.

The past could not be invaded by too much reality. 97 Danethorpe Vale had lodged itself firmly in that mysterious netherworld which was childhood memory. At future times the house might rise up in my consciousness and demand attention, however briefly; a plea that it should not be totally forgotten. One of those times was now, as if the house too had accepted that it and myself would never be physically reconnected, but wished, at this poignant moment, to offer up some small titbits for consideration.

Observational trivia this may be, but observations that would, before I close this book, better root the house and its other Mortimer occupants. They are fragments, fleeting glimpses, without logic or narrative progression, yet even in the act of writing them, I know they are important.

232

Here was our mother, bent over as she often was, not from age, but from being, despite the demands of her bladder, too busy to go to the toilet. Just one more task first, then perhaps another... Our mother rarely seemed to rest, scuttling about, her body contorted via this bladder constraint until the demands became too much, and brief time was taken out for the loo.

She rarely sat down to eat with the rest of us, instead hovered round the table, dishing up portions, then went back to the kitchen rattling pans, busying herself with we knew not what, while my father's exhortation "For heaven's sake Minnie, come and sit down!' went unheeded. At the meal's final moments she would tackle a plate of small morsels, less than half what she gave anyone else. For years I assumed all mothers ate like this.

On those rare occasions when the family went out for a pub lunch, mother usually plumped for nothing more indulgent than a cheese sandwich. She set every clock in the house forward ten minutes. She hoarded around a dozen two-pound bags of sugar in a kitchen cupboard,

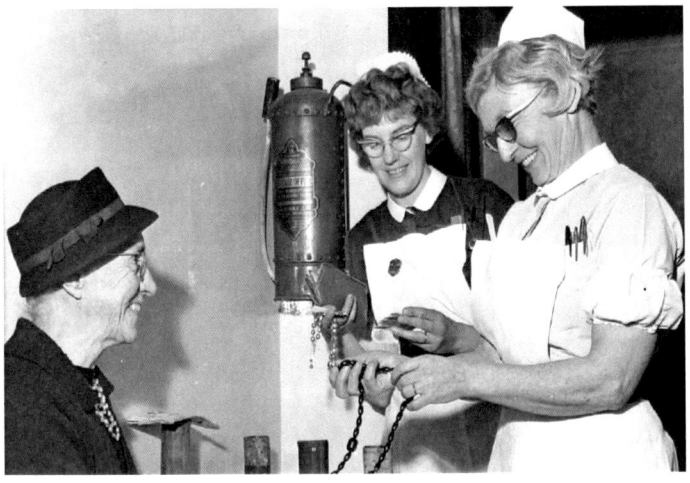

"Carry on Nurse" Minnie (right) as a sister in her City Hospital days, in Nottingham

233

though none of us had a sweet tooth. She used the same possum stick throughout my life. It moved with us from Sherwood Estate to Redhill. By the time she died it was as smooth and white as bone, and had shrunk to a few inches long. She imbued animals with unlikely talents with which she thought they attempted to outwit humans. Thus I heard her once refer to "that crafty goldfish!" She would fix cats or dogs with a critical stare.

Should the slightest drizzle begin, my mother would gaze from the window and dramatically exclaim that it was "raining cats and dogs!" Whenever my parents went on package holidays, even to the Southern Mediterranean, even in high summer, the first item she put in the suitcase was a hot water bottle.

She had a not oversympathetic attitude to the Mortimer side of the family. Thus any time one of her sons or her husband did anything that met with her disapproval, she would smack her forehead, toss her head in the air and mouth off the words, "Typical Mortimer!"

Like my father, and for reasons I never understood she disdained to use the past participle of the verb 'to eat'. Both would say, "Yesterday I eat a very nice sandwich." She often called me 'Alex' and my brother 'Peter'. This was life-long and seemed perfectly normal.

I have this strong audio memory of our father, how he would answer the phone with the one word, 'Mortimer', delivered with a portentous quality that immediately invested him with a certain gravitas. Later, I realised the pronouncing of this three-syllable single word, in a manner so unlike the normal style of speech on the estate, symbolically signalled an intention to free himself and his family from the constraints of our upbringing.

His first car was a tiny Ford Popular. In our last months before moving, his small business having taken off, he bought an old Jaguar which sat and preened itself outside on Danethorpe Vale — to the astonishment of the neighbours.

For my twenty-first birthday he gave me a £150

234

cheque, which he took back a few days later when I drove his company's Ford Zodiac to Manchester to see my brother at university, and blew it up — the car, not the university. The engine was a write-off.

When he established his own brand of knitwear, he called it Galbraith, his middle name, despite my efforts to persuade him to the name Mr Mort.

Each Sunday breakfast, with his knife, he would carefully scrape away the flesh from the grilled tomato, and eat it. A little later, when he wasn't looking, I would manage to wolf down the tomato skins.

I only ever once saw him drunk, at the age of seventy-eight, at a family gathering in Rotherham, when at midnight he stood up and shouted, 'Let's all go down the disco!' He was in bed ill for the next two days.

He once pretended to be the non-existent Lord Galbraith in order to secure a table for the family in a Dublin restaurant. At that moment I felt immensely proud of such rarely-seen playfulness.

When High Pavement Grammar School announced they were to keep me down a year because of slow development, he put in a personal and successful plea for a change of mind. His legs have been inherited by my son Dylan, who has also inherited his forearms.

And my brother Alex: at the age of eight, when I was six, Alex invented a character called Longchin who he would create by contorting his face and changing his voice. Longchin would talk to me at length. This occasional *alter ego* lasted at least a year. So effective was this metamorphosis, so convinced was I of the character's existence, that to this day I still find myself wondering as to Longchin's whereabouts.

Alex was probably the only person on Sherwood Council Estate to have A-levels in Ancient Greek and Latin. He could recite by heart the full Ancient Greek alphabet. He played left-wing at football, and was pretty good. His hero was the Leicester City centreforward and record goal scorer Arthur Rowley, and for some reason Leicester City FC was

235

always his team, not County or Forest. No-one else I knew in Nottingham supported Leicester.

Both of us were school boxing champions. Both of us were among the school's best long-distance runners. He was always the cleverest in his class, and sailed through exams, which made me envious, because I floundered. He was the first person I knew from the estate to read *The Guardian*. If someone wanted to know anything, we'd say, "Ask Alex". On the telephone we sounded identical, and still do.

Unlike the rest of the family, he had curly hair.

In our early gang, everyone adopted names from the *Oor Wullie* cartoon strip. Alex was Soapy. I was Wee Eck. To this day, my brother and his family call me Eck.

* * *

My partner Kitty was due to collect me later that day. A month had passed, and a lifetime. What had I learned about Valerie and Derrick?

I sat Valerie down and asked her some questions. This is what she said: "I came to Sherwood Estate in 1975 after my house in the Meadows area of Nottingham was demolished. I have four children by my former husband Ken: Veronica, Sylvia, Mark and Jason. I lived alone for a while then Derrick and I got together around 1998. There is another family connection in that Derrick's daughter Cheri lives with my nephew Wayne, and they have a nine-year-old called Kate. I was a primary school teacher but some years ago took a month off with stress and never went back. I'm quite a stressful person. People don't mix so much these days, and I don't see myself as a particularly sociable person either."

I begged to disagree. Had she not allowed a total stranger to come and live in their house for a whole month? Did that not qualify for sociability?

"Possibly," she answered, and then, "I suppose the idea just sounded interesting."

236

I also invited Derrick to sit down for a few basic questions. During this session he imitated a jack-in-the box, constantly jumping up to do something; he got up and walked about, he picked up and read the newspaper, he switched on the television, and eventually he asked, "Is that it then?" It *was* it, and I'd written nothing down, and that was the nature of it.

I gathered up my worldly possessions from the room that had been a study, bedroom and bolthole for a month. As I did with all rooms that sheltered me for however long, I thanked it and bade it farewell.

Kitty arrived and we strapped the bike to the roof rack. On our return it would make an unexpected present for a writer mate.

We drove off the estate with Valerie and Derrick waving us goodbye from the gate; that inevitable sad sense of departure, of another chapter closed, was, I suspect, felt as much by them as myself. They had cared for me splendidly. As Kitty and I drove past 97 Danethorpe Vale, my glance was as cursory as I could make it.

POSTSCRIPT

I came to this book with little idea or masterplan, realising slowly that I was apprehensive of writing excessively about the past. This was due partly to the fact that, even given the unlikely event anyone would want to read the same, I'd never been attracted to writing an autobiography. For me, an author's life is not something to be recorded, more occasionally to be quarried, reshaped, redefined, made almost unrecognisable if needs must. I liked the idea of the author as alchemist whose magic would be dulled were he or she to use an excess of reality.

Not that we could define reality. There is no truth, only interpretation. Any so-called 'factual' event could be described a dozen different ways by a dozen different people.

As a writer, I had travelled to my past not just in the mind, but as a physical concrete journey, plonking myself down in the very same streets of my adolescence. I was glad to have done it, but also glad it was over. The journey had produced a strange cocktail of past and present, and not one I could always easily swallow.

If the past was another country, it was even more so when you left it so far behind, then physically returned, not for a fleeting visit, when you could hang on to delusions, and temporal distortions, but for a full month, when you couldn't.

Even writing this now, Sherwood Council Estate risks sliding back into the 1950s and early 60s, attempting to shoulder out my recent time there.

Which is natural, for that era *was* my real time on the estate, when it was my natural hunting ground, when for better or worse, it formed the adolescent Mortimer. Thereafter, again for better or for worse, I was re-formed, made anew.

238

And yet, unlike the Alan Sillitoe or D.H. Lawrence novels, this is not a book that could have been written from a distance.

To write it, I had to return to, and to feel, for one month, the city's well-known but also unfamiliar embrace. At times this embrace suffocated me, other times I feared it, misunderstood it, or wanted nothing more than to be a million miles from its pervasive presence.

I admired a writer such as David Almond, a personal friend, whose working-class Tyneside childhood has been alchemically transformed in a series of brilliant young people's novels from *Skellig* onwards. Almond's imagination, his ability to create such vivid, often fantastical fiction from the basic raw material of a working-class childhood on 'The Felling' estate, proves that magic can be forged from the most unlikely circumstances.

My own acknowledgement to my home town is far less ambitious. And yet in a strange way, there's a sense of a duty fulfilled, an obligation carried out, as if somehow in my writer's life, I needed to reconnect with Nottingham, and to discover exactly where this reconnection led. Which is what has happened. I feel the city and I are now on a different level. There's a sense of relief, such as that felt by a couple who finally sit down to discuss long-avoided but important aspects of their relationship.

And I understand the inevitability of my sense of alienation on Sherwood Estate. Part of this understanding came when, some weeks after returning home, I picked up the book of work by the painter George Shaw, *The Sly and Unseen Day,* which I'd bought prior to my visit.

Just before Nottingham I went to see Shaw's exhibition at The Baltic, Gateshead (the painter was later shortlisted for the 2012 Turner Prize). All the painter's distinctive works depicted Tile Hill Estate in the West Midlands, where the painter grew up as a teenager. Unusually, he paints in Humbrol enamel, and even more unusually, not a single human figure appears in these urban paintings. The streets of this council estate are hauntingly empty, houses are often shuttered, pubs closed down, we stare along graffitied alleyways, view a deserted playing field with broken goalposts, one painting has the deliberately unromantic title *Landscape with Dog Shit Bin.* Even when the houses look neat and tidy, as in the painting *Ash Wednesday,* the well cared-for scene lacks a single human being.

I'd looked at the book pre-Nottingham, but looking post-Nottingham produced another epiphany moment, and the realisation that Shaw (though much younger than me) underwent a similar journey. He could paint this estate, its physicality, its geographical reference points. He'd grown up with them. Yet the sense of sadness and melancholia, as with myself, was obvious. What he could not do in all honesty as an artist was paint the council estate's people, for they were now strangers to him, just as the people on Sherwood Estate were strangers to me. Shaw's dichotomy was similar to my own. We had both returned to our childhood estate, and excised the estate people. He could as soon paint the current estate dwellers, as I could spend time knocking on doors and interviewing them. There was not any evidence that Shaw had any interest in tracking down the people he knew during his estate youth. Me neither.

Books discussed in *Made in Nottingham*

Skellig	David Almond
Bone & Cane	David Belbin
City of Crime	(Ed.) David Belbin
Bring Back the Birch	Alan Birchenall
The History of Sherwood	Tony Fay
This Gun for Hire	Graham Greene
Lonely Hearts	John Harvey
Robin Hood	J.C. Holt
The Rainbow	D.H. Lawrence
Sons and Lovers	D.H. Lawrence
Women in Love	D.H. Lawrence
Stuck up a Tree	Jenny McLeod
Steak Diana Ross	David McVay
A Short Answer	Stanley Middleton
Harris's Requiem	Stanley Middleton
A Cautious Approach	Stanley Middleton
England's Greatest Traitor	Ian Mortimer
Sleepwalking	Julie Myerson
Captain of Hungary	Ferenc Puskás
The Sly and Unseen Day	George Shaw
Saturday Night and Sunday Morning	Alan Sillitoe
Start Somewhere	Michael Standen
The Day of the Triffids	John Wyndham

ACKNOWLEDGMENTS

With thanks to: Valerie and Derrick for being there, Eileen Jones for extra proof-reading, Carol Clewlow for unearthing a rare Graham Greene copy, Ross Bradshaw for indulging my idiosyncrasies, Kitty Fitzgerald for the car and all the many other forms of support, Jill Clarke for late night listening, Sheila Reid for reconnecting me with lost Mortimers, David Belbin for the books.